Walk Like You Have
Somewhere to Go

4/17

To Connie,

thanks so much!

Lucille

Walk Like You Have Somewhere to Go

My Journey from Mental Welfare
to Mental Wealth

Lucille O'Neal

with Allison Samuels

NELSON
BOOKS

An Imprint of Thomas Nelson

Published in Nashville, Tennessee, by Nelson Books, an imprint of Thomas Nelson. Nelson Books and Thomas Nelson are registered trademarks of HarperCollins Christian Publishing, Inc.

Page design by Walter Petrie.

Thomas Nelson, Inc., titles may be purchased in bulk for educational, business, fund-raising, or sales promotional use. For information, please e-mail SpecialMarkets@ThomasNelson.com.

Unless otherwise indicated, Scripture quotations are taken from the HOLY BIBLE: NEW INTERNATIONAL VERSION®. © 1973, 1978, 1984 by International Bible Society. Used by permission of Zondervan Publishing House. All rights reserved.

Scripture quotations marked CEV are taken from THE CONTEMPORARY ENGLISH VERSION. © 1991 by the American Bible Society. Used by permission.

Scripture quotations marked ESV are taken from THE ENGLISH STANDARD VERSION. © 2001 by Crossway Bibles, a division of Good News Publishers.

Scripture quotations marked KJV are taken from the King James Version of the Bible.

Scripture quotations marked NASB are taken from the NEW AMERICAN STANDARD BIBLE®. © The Lockman Foundation 1960, 1962, 1963, 1968, 1971, 1972, 1973, 1975, 1977. Used by permission.

Scripture quotations marked NKJV are taken from THE NEW KING JAMES VERSION. © 1982 by Thomas Nelson, Inc. Used by permission. All rights reserved.

Scripture quotations marked NRSV are taken from the NEW REVISED STANDARD VERSION of the Bible. © 1989 by the Division of Christian Education of the National Council of the Churches of Christ in the U.S.A. All rights reserved.

ISBN 978-1-59555-249-5 (PBD)

Library of Congress Cataloging-in-Publication Data

O'Neal, Lucille.
    Walk like you have somewhere to go : my journey from mental welfare to mental wealth / Lucille O'Neal ; with Allison Samuels.
        p. cm.
    ISBN 978-1-59555-307-2
    1. O'Neal, Lucille—Mental health. 2. O'Neal, Shaquille. 3. Self-esteem in women. 4. Basketball players—United States—Family relationships. I. Samuels, Allison. II. Title.
GV884.O54O54 2010
796.323092—dc22
    [B]   2009048773

Printed in the United Sates of America

11 12 13 14 15 WC 5 4 3 2 1

This book and memoir is dedicated to my earthly parents, Odessa Chambliss and Sirlester O'Neal, and my grandparents Hilton and Cillar O'Neal, who now watch over me from above. In their own special way, they helped me realize that I had something special deep inside of me to be shared with the rest of this world.

I also dedicate this book to my only brother, Roy, and my younger sisters, Vivian and Velma, for always being there for me through thick and thin and in good times and bad. There are not enough ways for me to show you how much I love you.

And last, I dedicate this memoir to my four beautiful children: Shaquille, Lateefah, Ayesha, and Jamal—the truest lights of my life.

Trust in the LORD with all thine heart; and lean not unto
thine own understanding. In all thy ways acknowledge
him, and he shall direct thy paths.

—Proverbs 3:5-6 KJV

Contents

Foreword by Shaquille O'Neal

There's not a doubt in my mind that at around 8 a.m. on March 6, 1972, I had my first opportunity to gaze into the eyes of an angel. I couldn't have asked for a more perfect image as my first sight after arriving in the world that day. Her name was Lucille, and I've had the pleasure of calling her Mother for the last thirty-eight years.

What can I say about the woman who's inspired me at every step of my own journey in the NBA and beyond? She gave up so much for me and my brother and sisters so that we could have opportunities and lifestyles none of us could have ever dreamed of. Certainly, years ago, as we moved around from place to place with my father, Phil (who was in the Army), we never imagined all of what we have been able to achieve.

Because my mom was just a teenager when I was born, we supported each other as we both grew and evolved over the years. I remember how hard she worked as a single mother, and then as a wife and caretaker to a houseful of rambunctious (my sisters), stubborn (my brother), and well-behaved (me) kids. LOL!!

We never saw her down—she wouldn't allow it—and she balanced our lives, as well as her own, with the precision of a well-skilled neurosurgeon. She certainly kept me away from the lure of drug dealers in our neighborhood and off street corners as a young man so that I could realize my dream of playing professional basketball. Through it all, she's never let me give up on myself, even when things seemed the most hopeless.

Today, after my eighteen years in the NBA, she's still the ultimate inspiration for everything I do. Watching her have the courage to make life-altering decisions, such as returning to school after age forty, and becoming single again after twenty-eight years of marriage, has given me the strength to face my opponents (and anything else) both on and off the court with little hesitation.

I am what I am, and I have what I have, because of Lucille O'Neal's DNA running through my veins. Trust me—all who read this book will benefit from the wisdom I've been relying on for years. Thank you, Mommy! I love you.

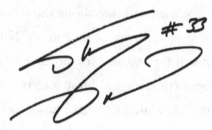

Preface

"While I have your attention" is a phrase that comes to mind sometimes when I take a moment to think about the last few years. My life, and for the most part the lives of my entire family, have been in the spotlight since the day my son Shaquille entered the NBA back in 1992. As far back as then, I've thought off and on about telling my own story. My life has always consisted of much more than just being the mother of a beloved sports icon or the recipient of massive fortune and fame.

Oddly enough, throughout the years I'd always convince myself that it wasn't the right time. Even recently I've questioned whether anyone really wanted to hear what a fifty-six-year-old New Jersey girl had to say. Why would they care? My thinking baffled Shaquille, who would regularly remind me of how inspiring my life's tale could be for the countless people out there facing the same obstacles and setbacks in their lives that I've faced in mine. My son even coined the term "mental welfare" for this book as a way of describing where

Walk Like You Have Somewhere to Go

I'd been emotionally at certain points in my life. Shaquille is my oldest child, and there is a six-year age difference between him and his next sibling. So for several years it was just the two of us trying to make it, which gave Shaquille—more than any of my other children—a front row seat to some of my darkest hours. Obviously, my son knows a good story when he lives one. Still, I hesitated to share my life in print. In hindsight, I realize that I hesitated because my story really didn't have all the necessary chapters until very recently. I had to come full circle with life's big events—like death, divorce, and renewal—before I could not only explain to people the meaning of my journey, but also how I'd come out on the other end and how they could do the same.

Today, after a very long and successful career in the NBA, my son is nearing the end of his time on the court. His retirement will more than likely also mark the end of much of the attention and fascination the public has had with his personal life—something I can honestly say I'm looking forward to. But it also hit me that the right time for me to lay it all out has finally arrived—the ups and downs and ins and outs of a life forever changed by a miracle, but still in progress—all "while I have your attention."

CHAPTER 1

"Living in Confusion"

Train up a child in the way he should go:
and when he is old, he will not depart from it.

—Proverbs 22:6 (KJV)

When I stepped through the door of our three-story New Jersey home that bright Summer afternoon, I knew my secret was a secret no more. On our deep-beige, plastic-covered sofa in the living room sat my mother, Odessa, smiling pleasantly as usual, and my grandmother Cillar, who (per usual) was not smiling at all. These two women were not the best of friends. In fact, they were far from it, which explained why they were sitting on opposite ends of the sofa. But something had brought them together on this fateful evening, and I was pretty sure it wasn't high tea. The two most prominent women in my world were there to confront me about something I'd chosen to ignore. In the previous weeks my seventeen-year-old body had begun to change ever so slightly.

I'd been skin and bones most of my young life, but suddenly I was putting on weight. My mornings before I departed for school were filled with constant trips to the bathroom to throw up, and nothing I ate stayed down for very long. These were all symptoms of a condition I was much too scared to even admit to myself was possible. This was 1971, not long after the end of the civil rights movement, and still a time when being young, single, and pregnant was a thing of shame for the entire family. To add to my disgrace, I'd been raised in the most Christian of households, so my embarrassment would be all the worse. How could I have sinned like that? my grandmother asked with absolutely no patience for my answer. Her disapproving face said it all. I was crushed and ashamed that day, but this is exactly how the impending birth of my oldest child, Shaquille Rashaun, was announced at my home. Though I knew his arrival would change my life forever, I never guessed in just how many mind-boggling ways.

As I sat there that day, listening to my grandmother lash out at me for all my "sinful transgressions," I did what I often do when things became too much for me to handle: I zoned out. Why would I stay in that moment to hear my grandmother accuse me of being a ho' on wheels and a tramp and any other negative name she could think of? In retrospect, I think my grandmother was angry about a lot of things that day—things that had little to do with me. Her life hadn't exactly been rainbows and moonbeams, and I'd unwittingly provided her a perfect opportunity to unleash all that pent-up frustration on me. My mother, on the other hand, said nothing as my grandmother verbally let loose. Her pleasant facial expression and smile said to be calm and let my grandmother vent. I tried my best to comply and just sat there with my hands folded in my lap. To stop myself from crying, I bit my lip and focused on a small piece of wallpaper that had begun to peel away behind my grandmother's head.

Many of the questions my grandmother asked me that day, she already knew the answers to. She most certainly had met my boyfriend and the father of my baby, because he'd been at the house a number of times. She even liked him, or at least she seemed to. Still, she felt it necessary to go over all the details of how I could have gotten myself in the "family way." She wanted reasons that day, but I had none for her. None that I wanted to share, that is. All I could manage to do was mumble I was sorry a thousand times, until I couldn't say it anymore and didn't want to say it again.

We never know where the circumstances of our lives, good or bad, will lead us. Lord knows I sure didn't. I was so depressed prior to Shaquille's birth. I felt my life was essentially over before it had a chance to begin. I was seventeen years old and just finishing high school when I found out I was pregnant. How would I rebound from having a baby so early in my life with no higher education or job skills? What kind of mother would I be when I was barely able to take care of myself? These questions haunted me prior to my son's birth and sent me spiraling down into a world of self-pity and self-doubt. But in truth, I knew my self-esteem issues didn't begin with Shaquille's future entrée into the world. I'd battled with the residue of an unloving and unhappy childhood for years, which in turn caused me to look for love in all the wrong places. But thirty-eight years ago I had no idea how to deal with the many confusing thoughts and feelings running through my young mind. I just knew I was heading in the wrong direction and needed to turn around before it was too late.

We don't often see in our childhoods many things that are blatant to us as adults. I can't keep count of the number of people who have told me they never knew they were poor growing up until they were fully grown. Honestly, I wish I'd been that clueless about my own life. I unfortunately understood very early on that I wasn't growing up in what anyone would call a "traditional family" setting—it wasn't even close. My parents divorced when I was just three years old, and that left my older brother, Roy; younger sister, Vivian; and me to be raised by my father and his family.

The fact that my parents separated when I was very young impacted my life in ways that I can't begin to fully comprehend, not even today. That single event would go on to define how I felt—in both positive and negative ways—about the woman I would later become. Obviously, many people go through divorce and learn to deal with the aftermath of a family torn apart; however, for me and my two siblings, there were so many questions about what actually happened to our family and why. These are questions that wouldn't be answered until much later on.

※

CHAPTER 2

Life Ain't Been No Crystal Stair

"For I know the plans I have for you,"
declares the LORD, "plans to prosper you and not to
harm you, plans to give you hope and a future."

—Jeremiah 29:11

Though I was born in a little town called Dublin, Georgia, I have absolutely no memories of the Deep South or of the home where I most likely took my first steps. As soon as our parents went their separate ways in the late 1950s, my father and his family moved us by car to Newark, New Jersey. I can still vaguely recall sitting in a jam-packed car for what seemed like forever as we made our way up north. Neither my brother and sister nor I could even ask if we were there yet because we didn't know where "there" was! Looking back at how hastily we moved to our new city, it almost feels as though my father's family wanted to make sure our earliest memories of life and our mother were erased as quickly as they had been formed.

Much later, my siblings and I would learn that we were moved to New Jersey so quickly because our mother wanted out of her marriage with our father. All I remembered during this time was that I didn't understand why our family wasn't like every other family I knew. All of the other families had a home with a mommy, a daddy, and children all living under one roof. There were always two parents, and certainly none of these families were moving to a new state to get away from each other. Nowadays it's more common than not that children grow up in a single-parent household, but this was a time in African-American life when two parents in the home was a given. How things have changed today, and unfortunately for the worse.

My family was different. When my father, brother, sister, and I first moved to Jersey (most of my father's family already lived in New Jersey), we shared the second floor of a crowded three-story building on South Eighth Street. Our differences from other families in the neighborhood didn't end there, mind you; my grandfather's brothers and sisters and their families also lived in that big building on Eighth Street: some on the first floor, more on the second floor with us, and the rest on the third floor. It's amazing the things I can still visualize all these years later, like the elaborate sleeping plan created for all of us to fit on that cramped second floor. In all honesty, it wasn't just people that made our new home so cramped. My grandparents loved the antique pieces of the time and had a great deal of large, dark, mahogany wood furniture throughout the house, that people pay an arm and leg for today. Of course, it wasn't that expensive back then, so anyone with any type of money furnished their homes that same way. For some reason that furniture always brought a certain melancholy and sadness to the house because it was so heavy, hard, and cold. There was no way to escape it either—because it was everywhere, in the hallway, the living room, and the bedrooms.

In fact, those pieces were so depressing to me that when I began furnishing my most recent house (or "little hut," as I like to call it), I made a point of only choosing light, mellow-colored sofas, chairs, etc.—in creams, tans, and yellow tones. Those colors always seem to calm, comfort, and relax me after a day out and about. Today, I love to complement my furniture with luscious green plants and colorful flowers. I love greenery, particularly since it was a luxury we couldn't afford when I was a child.

Not surprisingly, our little home in New Jersey soon became so overcrowded that we eventually had no choice but to move again. We packed up all of our belongings, and this time we moved into a larger abode at 296 Littleton Avenue. In this setup, our father slept on the couch in the living room, an aunt slept on a foldaway bed in the den, and another had a small bedroom near the front of the house. My sister and I shared one bed in a very, very small room in the front of the house. When I say small, I mean shoe-box tiny—we had to step outside of the room to turn around, and that's no joke. The full-size bed and mismatched tiny dresser (which my grandparents purchased from the Goodwill) that was placed in the corner took up every ounce of space. When Shaquille was born, we had to move the dresser out to fit his little crib in. As my sister and I got older, we craved our own space, but in the beginning it wasn't that bad being so close, literally and figuratively, to my sister. I was the oldest, so I could boss her around a little, and we could share things about our day that only sisters can. Having a little sister can drive you crazy, but it can also be a relationship like no other. My brother bunked near my father, and my grandparents shared the biggest bedroom in the home, all the way in the back on the second floor. Simply put, there were a whole lot of people in that house, and way too much thought had to be put into who went where.

Yet somehow we all managed to live together without anyone suffering any bodily harm. Now, that's not to say there weren't issues—trust me, there were a whole host of them that gradually wore me out as I began to get older and long for my own room. To complicate matters, as the middle child I always felt it was up to me to keep my brother and sister in line and in check. Go figure. This was no doubt the beginning of my lifelong trait of wanting to take care of everyone I loved. I wanted to keep peace in every situation, whether it was actually possible or not. This could simply have been the pattern of any middle child in a big family, but whatever the case, the self-imposed responsibility weighed heavily on me.

Lucille at five years of age in December 1959. Isn't she lovely?

It was my job, or so I convinced myself it was, to display a calm exterior at all times at home so things could run smoothly with my grandparents, who were exceedingly strict. No ifs, ands, or buts about it, it was their way or the highway, and it was a complete waste of time to argue otherwise. I imagine my grandparents were no different from many older people of their generation, particularly African Americans, who were just fighting to stay alive in many instances. It was their generation who had witnessed firsthand that not following the rules had the potential to get you into some serious trouble. But their strictness was sometimes very suffocating to us as young kids, and it negated a certain level of warmth I think all children need to feel confident and thrive.

I knew even back then that if I ever had my own kids, things would be entirely different. I'd give my children all the love they could handle, and then some. In fairness, now that I am older, I realize that distant love was probably the only type of love my grandparents knew how to give. In fact, it probably was how they were treated as children themselves. I can't imagine there were many occasions for hugs and kisses from their own parents at a time when African Americans were still being hung from trees and forced to work out in the fields. My grandparents were the descendants of slaves, who didn't or couldn't show affection because they feared they would become too emotionally attached to a loved one or a child who could soon be sold away. So understandably, our grandparents' attitude was that keeping us warm, fed, and safe *was* showing us all the love we needed.

It wasn't enough for me.

CHAPTER 3

Man About Town

Light dawns in the darkness for the upright;
he is gracious, merciful, and righteous.

—Psalm 112:4 (ESV)

My grandparents, Cillar (Mama) and Hilton O'Neal (Papa), were like a wrestling tag team in my life and in the lives of all my relatives and anyone else who knew them. They could deliver a serious one-two punch that could blindside you and knock you out before you ever knew what hit you. Although they worked quite effectively as a pair, it was without a doubt my grandfather's hovering presence that kept us all honest and on track. To know Hilton O'Neal was to respect him. He was a man who carried himself with a purpose and a plan no matter where he was. A physically striking man at a little over six feet tall, his deep, dark, chocolate complexion was as smooth as a newborn baby's skin, and boy, could he dress. Spectator shoes, perfectly pressed zoot suits, and fedora hats were his signature pieces, and he wore them with style and pride. My grandfather was one bad brother!

My grandfather Hilton and my grandmother Cillar (my father's parents). Aren't they a fine couple?

As a child, I viewed my grandfather with both awe and fear, never fully comprehending what it must have been like to be a black man full of confidence and swagger in those trying days. This was a time when African Americans were considered less than human, attacked by police dogs, and forced to sit in the back of the bus. Looking his best was the one way he could consistently show the world that he was a proud, full-fledged human being—no matter if the law disagreed. Many African-American males did the same during that time in an attempt to prove to the outside world that they were worthy of respect. It saddens me to see many of our young men today dress so sloppily, with sagging pants and an overall unkempt appearance. I often wonder if they truly understand how their ancestors, like my grandfather, took so much pride in looking their best and what it meant to them to be viewed as respected citizens. Presenting a well-kept look afforded them the chance to be at least recognized in a world where they were often dismissed.

My grandfather also had other talents that went against the grain of what African Americans were supposed *to be capable of* doing in those days. Though he worked in construction during the day, laying bricks and drywalling alongside his brothers and other family members, he had a sharp mind for business and owned several properties, even a neighborhood tavern and bar. His keen business savvy meant there was always food on our table and that we never went without—even during the days of profuse poverty for blacks. While my grandfather was too humble to talk about his own endeavors or his advanced entrepreneurial skills, his middle brother, Chappell, enjoyed nothing more than sitting in a big chair and detailing the early exploits of the O'Neal family for hours on end. "Uncle Chap," as we affectionately called him, was the self-appointed griot (African storyteller) of the family, and while his tales kept us quite entertained, we weren't always certain they were completely true.

Grandfather Hilton O'Neal in his later years Papa didn't take no mess!

The one story he just loved to tell year after year was how the O'Neal brothers were run out of Georgia when my grandfather and his brothers were young adults. According to Uncle Chap, the O'Neal boys were working as sharecroppers, just as many African Americans did back in those days. As sharecroppers, a black family grew seasonal fruits, vegetables, and other crops—such as cotton, corn, etc.—for the white landowners in exchange for a small piece of the profits and a place to stay. They would often sell the food at the farmers' markets and collect the money to pass on. At least that was the way it was supposed to be. My grandfather and his brothers had other ideas and were skillfully and quietly skimming money off the top from the money supposedly due the owners of the neighborhood sharecropping business. Translation: they were stealing money from the white people in town! That's how the entire O'Neal family ended up in New Jersey; they were busted and had to leave Georgia immediately with little more than the clothes on their backs.

My brother, sister, and cousins listened to this story countless times with the carefree wonderment of clueless children. We already knew our grandfather was fearless, so this only added to the myth of Hilton O'Neal in our eyes. Still, our grandfather's colorful history didn't lessen the impact of the coldness he and our other family members showed us at times.

Their often harsh reaction to us, especially me, caused me to bend over backwards to be what I thought was the "perfect little girl." This, of course, was not possible, because children will be children. But I was so afraid of disappointing my grandparents that I spent most of my young life under their roof second-guessing every action I took.

Even though I was just five years old at the time, I clearly remember my main concern was staying out of trouble and remaining in my grandparents' good graces at all costs. That meant never getting my clothes dirty at school or even having a hair out of place. Please remember, those were the days when parents spanked their children for the least little thing, so we all lived in total fear of the belt. And trust me; I received more than my share of whippings back then at the hands of my grandparents. They were painful spankings that sometimes left marks on my little body for days. One that instantly comes to mind happened on the day when my grandfather held me upside down by my legs and whipped me for what seemed like forever. I think I was ten years old, and for the life of me, I can't remember what I'd done. I do remember my legs hurting for days afterward. Physical punishment like that would be considered child abuse today.

This was the origin of what I came later to call my "mental welfare." I realize the term *mental welfare* has a disturbing and complicated essence to it. Let me explain what it actually means as it applies to me. In my life, mental welfare was defined by the absence of self-love and resulted in a total lack of self-esteem and confidence. I realize this is a definition for a feeling that many women and men go through every day in their lives—but I desperately needed to put a name with the "disease."

And it was a disease. My symptoms were made all the worse as a child because I often heard many of the negative things said by my father's family about our mother when she wasn't around to hear or defend herself. They said mean and vicious things, suggesting that she didn't want us and that she'd left us behind in the divorce. Now, let's be clear; even though my memory of my mother was slim at best, I didn't believe this for one second, and no amount of talking was going to convince me otherwise. Nonetheless, it hurt to hear; no child wants to think that one of their parents just threw them away one day. I was soon to find out the truth.

CHAPTER 4

"We Are Family"

"I will be a Father to you, and you will be my sons
and daughters, says the Lord Almighty."

—2 Corinthians 6:18

There are no words to describe what an incredible feeling it is for me to sit in the stands of a sold-out arena and watch Shaquille play the game of basketball. The excitement of the crowd each time he gets his hands on the ball is enough to make any mother beam with joy from ear to ear without fail. Though I've been watching my oldest son play the game on a professional level for a good eighteen years, hearing the crowd cheer and shout his name never gets old. Now that he has a new teammate in LeBron James and a new team in Cleveland, it's as though he's saved the best for last.

His games are, of course, nothing like the games I watched as a child back in New Jersey. Maybe because of the cruel stories my family would tell us, I spent many afternoons outside on our unpainted cobblestoned porch, watching other children play kickball in the vacant lot across the street. I never had the desire to join in. I'd just sit there and wonder how hard it must have been for our mother to have her children, her own flesh and blood, torn away from her with no say in the matter. I imagined how she must have cried at the thought of not having her babies with her to care for and love. As a mother, I'm sure she yearned for the chance to read us bedtime stories and tuck us in at night. I'm also sure she wanted to be there to kiss our bruises and scrapes and to wipe away our tears.

Those kinds of thoughts only increased years later, once I became a mother. Even as young as I was when Shaquille was born, the bond between mother and child was intact from the moment I saw his sweet little face looking up into my eyes at the hospital. I would have been forever traumatized if someone had taken him away from me for any reason. Those images haunted me for a long time, and they weren't exactly the thoughts that a child my age should have been saddled with.

When I was really riled up over my mother, I'd hash out my feelings with my brother, Roy, and my sister, Vivian, who agreed that there was no way our mother could have just left us. Since Roy was the oldest, he had the strongest memory of my mother, which was very strange for me. For some reason, I felt as though I'd known her just as long, if not longer, which made absolutely no sense, given our birth order.

My mother and I always had an unusually strong connection that was hard to explain, even before she reappeared in our lives later on. I like to think we had such a strong bond because our personalities were so similar. We both hated conflict of any kind, and we both worried constantly about other people's opinions of us. We both also felt that other people's happiness was always much more important than our own. Though I didn't know it then, this is exactly how mental welfare thrives and survives. Though she probably never gave it much thought, I think my mother suffered from some aspect of mental welfare as well. You give and give until there's nothing left to offer, and ultimately you pay a price for that type of vulnerability. Unfortunately, my mother paid a big price—her children were taken away from her. I wouldn't fully understand that until years later, when I paid a huge price in my own marriage.

Still, despite all the issues we were having with our grandparents, my brother, sister, and I still tried our best to become accustomed to our new home and new way of life. Not a very easy task given the dishonesty we were living with. During the first few months of living there with our grandparents, we were unaware that our mother had been trying for many months to reach us, and that our grandmother was turning her away each time she attempted to reach out. I'm not sure why I was surprised at my grandmother's actions. We called our grandmother "Mama," and she was certainly not an imposing figure in any type of physical way; in fact, I would be much taller than her for most of my life. But, man, did she possess a presence that screamed, "I'M THE BOSS AROUND HERE!"

Though she didn't put the fear of God in us like my grandfather, with just one word from her mouth, everyone in the house (no matter the room or the floor) would stop what they were doing, stand still, and just listen to her lash out at whoever she had a problem with that day. She was not a woman to be trifled with, and she made sure you knew it.

Grandmother Cillar O'Neal, possibly in 1965. She was a bad mamma jamma with her cat-eye glasses.

She and my grandfather legally adopted us after our parents divorced, and she let it be known that our mother coming into the mix would cause complications that she didn't need and wasn't going to deal with. We never knew what my father thought about our grandparents' gaining custody of us, but he didn't seem to object. I think he liked not having responsibility of any kind. We were all together anyway, so I can't imagine it was a big deal. Thankfully, our mother was a fighter, much more than I think my father's family gave her credit for. She never gave up on trying to find a way to get to us.

Her efforts finally paid off one day, two years after we'd left Georgia. We three kids were all sitting in the living room, watching our favorite TV show, *I Love Lucy*, when the telephone rang. Vivian, being the feisty, independent person she was then (and still is), raced toward the phone and answered it. It was our mother calling. Vivian couldn't believe it was her on the other end. How could she? She was just a year old when we separated from our mother. As my sister announced loudly who was on the line, my brother and I sprinted to the phone, worried our mother might somehow disappear before we had a chance to hear her voice again. Without a doubt, that one phone call was life changing for all three of us. We spent about ten minutes each, telling our mother what grade we were in, what our favorite subjects were in school, and what we wanted for Christmas that year. Our mother just laughed as we rattled on endlessly, seemingly thrilled at our full disclosure. Much to our grandparents' chagrin, that conversation dispelled any notion that we had been abandoned. Having our mother tell us she loved us, never stopped thinking about us, and certainly never deserted us forced our grandparents to change their negative tune and compelled them to allow our mother back into our lives.

In sharp contrast, we never had an idea what our father felt about our mother's returned presence in our lives. She had been the one to leave the marriage and end what was essentially our family. He couldn't have been pleased to have her reappear again in such a prominent way. But he showed no reaction to this major event, and said nothing, as he did with most things in our lives.

Me at age six trying to be that perfect little girl.

Though our grandparents were also less than pleased with our mother's refusal to just go away, after a few months of back-and-forth with her regarding how our new situation would play out, our grandparents finally and begrudgingly lifted their ban of our mother. Terms of when and where we'd visit our mother had to be ironed out before our grandparents actually gave the go-ahead. My grandmother would indeed have to have the last word, and no one was going to stop her. Our mother didn't let this deter her, of course. She'd waited too long to let a few details keep her from her children any longer. Our telephone calls with her gradually turned into our being given permission to visit her Jersey City, New Jersey, home a few times a month. She'd moved to New Jersey to live with some of her relatives shortly after we were taken away. That first weekend with our mother is a memory that still lingers in my mind like a beloved, favorite song. We rode the Trailways bus two hours to see her, and our hearts literally dropped when we saw her standing outside the station as soon as the bus turned the corner. She was clutching her purse, dressed in a navy blue suit with a matching pillbox hat, à la Jackie Kennedy. All that was missing were those signature gloves and the White House in the background. When we stepped off the bus, she met us each with long hugs and bunches of kisses. I was in heaven!

Now that I'm older, I am able to recognize that our mother's presence surely must have been an incredibly difficult situation for my grandparents to come to terms with. Their control over us had been successfully challenged, and though my mother would have little say in our day-to-day lives, her influence over us was undeniable from that very first phone call. Those weekends with our mother were pure magic, and it wasn't just because she didn't wake us up at the crack of dawn to go to church, like our grandparents. Church was an integral part of our grandparents' lives; it had gotten them through many a tough time in their day, and that translated into it being a mandatory place for us to be on Sunday and several other days during the week. Though I didn't realize it then, in retrospect, it provided a wonderful foundation to build my own faith on. But back then I didn't quite see it that way.

Our mother was also a woman of faith, but thanks to the Lord, as a treat, she'd let us sleep in on Sunday morning until we were ready to get up. Those weekends gave my brother and sister and me so much joy. All the love and nurturing we didn't receive from our grandparents, we got twofold from our mother. Our first weekend at her new apartment was also nerve-racking in some ways. Naturally, there was a lot of anticipation, because none of us really knew what to expect. How could we? We simply did not know our own mother. Of course, we had all these ideas of what we thought she'd be like, but with all the disparaging things said about her by our father's family, our little minds were totally confused. In truth, I think I put my mother on the tallest pedestal of all, much more than my siblings did. I was constantly fantasizing about how sweet she'd smell, how she styled her hair, what kind of clothes she wore, and how she'd probably bake us chocolate chip cookies every day if we lived with her. You know; all the wonderful things I thought good mothers did for their kids. It wasn't very realistic, but it was the mother any child longing for affection would conjure up in her young mind.

Odessa Chambliss in Jersey City in 1959. Our mother was beautiful, classy, and sweet as honey!

Thankfully, my mother wasn't far from the mark. In so many ways, her home was completely opposite that of our grandparents. It was just a small apartment, but it was comfortable, cozy, and full of life. And so was she. I like to think that I look a little like her. She had the most flawless mahogany complexion you could imagine—similar to Mahalia Jackson's beautiful skin—and she always wore a captivating scent. She loved smelling good, so she always wore a floral Avon perfume that lingered in the air long after she'd left the room. I still keep a bottle of that fragrance in my bedroom to remind me of her when I miss her the most. Always keeping her eye on the latest New York fashions, she dressed fabulously. But that was just on the outside. One-on-one she had the kindest, most gentle eyes and gave the type of hugs that made you never want to let go of her. Rules and regulations at her home weren't beaten into our heads every hour of the day.

For us, it was almost like escaping from prison and being just a short bus ride away from Disneyland. Isn't that what every child wants—to go to Disneyland?

CHAPTER 5

"Love, No Limit"

Love each other deeply,
because love covers over a multitude of sins.

—1 Peter 4:8

O ddly enough, my parents' divorce still saddens me to this day, even after all these years. I thought a great deal about both of my parents, and in particular my mother, last year, when my oldest daughter, Lateefah, married in a beautiful afternoon ceremony. Watching your child share vows with another person is a heart-tugging life moment, without doubt. Seeing my daughter with that amazing bridal glow, in her wedding gown, and really sensing the love she had with her new husband reminded me of what a happy union can mean for your life. My mother didn't have that with our father, and I know that hurt her desperately. She would have been so thrilled to see her granddaughter so beautiful and happy in a marriage that I pray will stand the test of time.

Somehow, despite all she'd been through, our mother was always the most patient person I'd ever met. She never failed to answer any and all of our questions, even the dumb ones kids always ask their parents. At such young ages—I was just five years old when we began to visit her, Roy was seven, and Vivian was only three— we didn't ask much about the divorce or about what happened between her and our father in prior years. It would be a while before any of us began to piece together what we could about our parents before they went their separate ways. At the time, we were just happy to spend time with her and to have a break from the stringent rules that governed my grandparents' home.

It seemed, at least to me, that our mother got married early in her life because she had to. Back in those days in the Deep South, when you reached a certain age as a woman, you were expected to be out of your family's home and into your own. But not as a single woman—oh no!! You had to be married, with your own home and family. This forced a great deal of young women, who more than likely were not ready for marriage at such young ages, to find partners quickly and without the benefit of getting to really know the other person well. Imagine if that were the thought process today. Think what limitations that would put on young women and their futures. What attracted my parents to each other is something I guess I will never know. On the surface it didn't look like they had very much in common beyond coming from the same hometown.

My father, Sirlester O'Neal (Daddy), was a hardworking, simple man with loads of integrity and pride. He suffered from a minor handicap that made it difficult for him to speak clearly. Not being able to communicate fully was particularly frustrating for him and hampered his learning process throughout his life. He was an adult before he was able to write well enough to sign his own name. I'm no doctor, but I've always felt that his anger over his handicap contributed to the demise of our parents' marriage. The rage he must have experienced being unable to do the simplest things must have had a profound impact on his personality and his interactions with all the people around him. How could you have a successful marriage when the most important aspect of it (communication) was nearly impossible?

My father, Sirlester O'Neal, was so cool and calm back in the day!

Today it's sad for me to think about the fact that there are now so many programs in place to handle minor handicaps like my father's. Speech therapy or just a little extra time with a teacher would have made a world of difference for him. That wasn't an option fifty years ago in Dublin, Georgia, and certainly not for a little country black boy. His disability robbed me, my brother, and my sister of a very important relationship, and to this day I live with that regret.

Our father's disability also explained why our grandmother was so protective of him. She spoke for him when he couldn't speak for himself, and she stood up for him when she thought someone was doing him wrong. I think that's one reason she fought so hard to make sure we were brought to New Jersey to live with them after our parents divorced. To have his wife leave him and then take his children would have been a double slap in my father's face, as it would be to any man. My grandmother wanted to salvage something from the marriage for him so he didn't feel powerless and alone.

In reality, my father had very little power. He had virtually no say in the way we were being raised or treated. In truth, he was as likely to get chastised by my grandmother for leaving something on the floor or not doing a chore as we were. Most of my childhood I basically thought of him as another sibling—a big brother, really. Because his speech was limited, we could never get privy to his true feelings or emotions about anything involving us or anyone else. We didn't know if it bothered him not to have a say in our development or growth. No, he was no huge fan of a lot of responsibility, but a man likes to be a man, and being under the thumb of your own parents as an adult had to be a tough pill to swallow. Sometimes, when I think about it today, I feel so bad for how useless our father must have felt as an adult man; unable to reveal his true emotions and prevented from reaching his full potential.

With time, I also began to connect the pieces of the puzzle on my own about my parents' marriage, and I concluded (I have no proof, mind you—just my own instincts) that our mother more than likely suffered from some sort of mental abuse or possibly physical abuse in the marriage. I realize how strong of a statement this is without actual proof. My mother would never speak ill of our father to us because she respected him too much. But the reality is, my father would have had no other way to express the anger he had bottled up inside. For many men back then, taking their frustrations out on their wives and other family members was a very normal thing. Neighbors looked the other way because it was so common it probably was happening on some level in their homes as well. Domestic violence wasn't even a term back then, and there were certainly no shelters or support groups to take women in who wanted to get out of a bad union. I think our mother took the abuse as long she could for our sakes, and then she just left. I would later find out how really difficult it can be to walk away when I was faced with a similar situation.

Ironically, my father turned into somewhat of a lady's man after he and my mother divorced. Though he didn't talk much, he was tall and slender, with what I guess you'd call a quiet charm that seemed to draw women in like magnets. Go figure! I always imagined he showcased a totally different personality when away from us. For all we knew, he could have been a regular chatterbox when he hit the bars at night.

My mother was a very different story. What you saw was what you got. To her credit, she didn't give up on love or life after losing her children and failing in her first marriage. She could have blamed herself for everything and just given up on a better and happier future. But she never stopped yearning for the life she knew she deserved or searching for a man she could love and truly be loved by.

My sister Velma was born shortly before my mother met and

married a wonderful man named Rhodes Chambliss. Rhodes was absolutely a godsend for all of us. He was tall with a light complexion and a low-cut Afro he wore all the time. He worked as a janitor at the experimental hospital in the city and treated our mother like the true queen she was. He didn't treat us too shabbily, either. What I really loved about him was that he lived to do only three things: work hard, drink at the bar, and take care of my mother. Such an amazing man! The stories I love to tell my kids are the ones where he'd bring home lab animals from the hospital for my mother to cook for dinner or for us to play with as pets. Until my mother told him to stop, that is. That was so much fun because we never knew what specimen he'd bring home, and we'd spend the entire day waiting and wondering. Another treat that our mother gave Vivian and me during those weekends away was paying a woman two dollars to hot-comb and style our hair. We felt like little divas, having such pampering as that.

Without fail, every Sunday, before we would head to the bus station to go back to our grandparents' house, Rhodes would pile us into his long, blue convertible to go for a ride in the city and to get ice cream cones. That adventure put a huge topping on an amazing two days. I still laugh at the memory of me, with my little bit of hair blowing in the wind, as we drove down the winding streets and busy turnpike in Jersey City. Earlier in the day (the last day of our weekend visit), instead of church we would spend the day going to stores to pick up new clothes and shoes that we might need for school. All we had to do was tell our mom or Rhodes what we needed for class and we got it with no fuss. Sadly, Rhodes died of cancer when Shaquille was only two years old. I'm so sorry my children never got to know him as a part of the family.

He was an easygoing, upstanding man, who made my mother very happy. She never remarried after his death.

Still, while things were wonderful on the weekends we were able to spend with our mother, we still spent the majority of our time with our grandparents, and that became increasingly stifling as we got older. The most difficult thing for me to deal with was that there was no freedom for me to be myself, or even attempt to find out who I was in the first place. Of course, I didn't know what the problem was back then; I just knew I was extremely unhappy, I felt unloved in many ways, and I was too ashamed to talk about it. To make matters worse, by the time I was nine or ten, I began sprouting upwards like a tree—literally. It was beyond baffling, because my father's family wasn't that tall. Yes, my dad was about six feet—but I was six feet by the time I was twelve. To my chagrin, my younger sister, Vivian, was growing at a normal rate and never made it past five foot eight. I just didn't understand, but I didn't resent her for it either. I just wanted my height to be normal as well.

My eighth grade graduation. I'm on the second from the top, in the checked suit and white headband.

I was also confused. Because of the lost connection with my mother and her family, we didn't find out anything, really, about her family until much later. They were primarily still located in the Deep South, worlds away from us. This disconnect wasn't exactly uncommon in many African-American families. I think it goes without saying that many in our community still know little about our distant relatives and their histories. So much was lost during the days of slavery and in the years afterward. Sometimes it was because the history wasn't recorded, or sometimes it was just too painful to relay. I was an adult before I realized that my mother's father was over seven feet tall. Although it would skip a generation or two, his great grandson, Shaquille, would later tower at seven foot one. But none of that future knowledge helped me in grade school as I dwarfed all the girls and boys in my class. Plus, many in my family felt quite comfortable telling me how unattractive I was. I really don't think they fully understood how painful their mean-spirited words were to me. They didn't understand the weight of words on a person's soul—my soul. To complete my misery, I weighed about a pitiful ninety-five pounds. Picture that for a minute—talk about awkward. You can imagine the fun the other kids had at my expense, given my looks. Children can truly be so cruel to others. Some were particularly mean, calling me names like "Jolly Green Giant" and "Olive Oyl" whenever I walked by. Their laughter cut me to the core. I wanted to tell someone how much I was hurting and how bad I felt about being so different from everyone else around me. But no one was listening.

Give thanks to the Lord, for he is good;
his love endures forever.

—1 Chronicles 16:34

CHAPTER 6

Can I Get an Amen?

He sent prophets to them . . . [but] they would not listen.

—2 Chronicles 24:19 (NASB)

My height continued to inch upward as my self-esteem continued to nosedive during my preteen years. But was anyone really paying attention to that in my house? No! How could they, when the O'Neal family life consisted primarily of school, work, and church? (And then church, church, and more church.) All day Sunday, Monday, Wednesday, Friday, and even Saturday was spent doing activities at St. Paul's Church of God in Christ. Be it prayer meeting, Bible study, choir practice, bake sales, or car washes—you name it—we were always there, seated on the front pew.

During those days, instead of spending time with my friends in the neighborhood, like most children my age, I was usually at church, cleaning up, performing my duties at Sunday school class (where I was the secretary), or doing whatever else had been assigned to me that week on the church grounds. Roy and Vivian were also with me, and they had their own assigned chores. My grandfather and grandmother were never far away as they did whatever was needed to keep the small church up and going. Papa was a respected deacon, Mama a deaconess, so they had to present a responsible front to the members. A few of my aunts and uncles also attended the church, while a few others attended another across town.

You can't imagine how I dreaded the sameness of that routine week after week. If there was any positive side to spending most of my time in the house of the Lord 24/7, it was our pastor, Rev. Iola Hartsfield. I so loved just hearing her name. She was one of the few female evangelists in the area, which made our church quite progressive in those days. Even today, female ministers are still few and far between in African-American churches, though the numbers do seem to be increasing.

For me, Rev. Hartsfield's very presence was mind-numbing. It was such an awesome vision back then to see this woman of color—so confident and sure of herself—in a man's profession and world. Her only focus was spreading God's Word and uplifting the people in her congregation and in the community. Watching this courageous woman command the attention of all her members with effortless skill and ease spoke volumes to me about what was possible. I'm pretty sure that's where I first got the idea in my head that one day I wanted to become a public speaker.

Rev. Hartsfield was not a physical powerhouse; she was nothing but a little bit of a woman. She couldn't have been more than knee-high to a duck, even with heels; but she stood like a giant among giants no matter where she was. I guess that's why she took such a special interest in me. As I mentioned before, I was already six feet

tall by my twelfth birthday! But I despised my height (and everything else about myself at that time), and because of it, I walked
slumped over with my head hanging down, trying my best to shrink
and go unnoticed. Rev. Hartsfield wasn't having it. She regularly
chastised me about my poor posture and lack of energy. Somehow,
I always felt that she was one of the few people in my life who could
tell how badly I was hurting on the inside. She seemed to see right
through me.

Though I tried to fight it, she also managed to bring out parts of
me that I never knew existed. One of my fondest childhood memories is of her (with her purse hanging in the crook of her arm) dem-
onstrating her signature no-nonsense strut down the aisle of the
church, with ten or twelve of us girls struggling to follow behind
her. That vivid image makes me laugh at myself to this day—and I
can still do that feisty walk!

Rev. Hartsfield also gave many of us young people assignments
to moderate services on alternating Sundays. Those assignments
usually included reading church announcements, welcoming visi-
tors, and giving special presentations during the order of service.
For me, the very thought of standing up in front of all of those
people made my stomach do flip-flops. I had been teased so much
about my looks that I couldn't imagine why she'd suggest such a
thing. How would I look? Would my hair look okay? I took great
pride in making sure every hair on my head was in place at all
times. I didn't have a lot of hair, mind you, but what I did have
needed to be just right. My favorite hairstyle involved bangs—
always bangs, until I got into high school and embraced a very
stylish Afro—which had to have a perfect uniform curl, achieved
with those infamous pink foam rollers that girls still use today.

Then I'd worry about whether my dress was ironed perfectly, if my shoes were right, and whether people would notice I looked just like a giant beanstalk standing up there in front of everyone.

How I got through those Sunday programs, I honestly don't know, but it was a challenge Rev. Hartsfield obviously felt I was up to. This determined woman didn't stop with just putting me in front of the congregation. She also found it necessary to try to uplift me from her place in the pulpit. I will never forget one Sunday morning when she actually spoke directly to me with the words, "Lucille, walk like you have somewhere to go." Given my intense shyness (and desire to be absolutely invisible) her acknowledgment of me in front of everyone was mortifying. People turned to look at me, and I felt like I couldn't sink down in the pew far enough to escape their probing stares. It would be years before I understood what this remarkable lady was trying to do for me and for my confidence. But at the moment she did it, all I knew was that I wanted to die of embarrassment.

For as long as I remained active in the church, Rev. Hartsfield continued to have an undeniable influence on me. Even after I no longer attended St. Paul's Church, I continued to flash back to the words she'd spoken to motivate me during my developmental years. Rev. Hartsfield lived to be nearly one hundred years old, and though she no longer is on this earth, a part of her still lives very much inside of me.

As I reached my teenage years, the dynamics of my family began to change rapidly, and with that came several life-altering events that would shape me well into the future. Like most teenagers, those transitional years from childhood to young adulthood transported me deeper into my own private funk. I internalized every look, frown, and cross word from anyone as confirmation that I wasn't worthy. I'd think, *If only I were shorter, cuter, or smarter, I'd be happier.* That was that good old mental welfare in full effect once again.

By the time I turned fourteen, Grandfather Hilton had become ill with diabetes and had slowly begun to lose his strength and ability to get around. In truth, he'd probably been sick and suffering years before (his heavy drinking didn't help), but in those days the older generation never complained about what ailed them. They worked hard day after day until they could work no more, never letting on to what their disease or illness was doing to them. That description fit my grandfather to a T. For as long as I could remember, his larger-than-life presence was the mainstay of our home. He was the one who made it all come together; he kept the dogs at bay. It was as if he had magical powers that made him invincible; at least that's how it seemed to my young mind.

Watching the tall, strapping man, whose voice used to put fear in my heart just by calling my name, slowly waste away was more heartbreaking than I can explain. Once he was hospitalized, I would go up to visit him and clip his fingernails and toenails to make him more comfortable while he slept. I just wanted to do something to ease his pain for however long he had left. When he died, it felt like the whole world just stopped rotating on its axis, without warning.

Despite the fact that we'd had a complicated relationship for most of my life, I did love my grandfather very much. Yes, he was sometimes distant, cold, and way too hard on us as children, but he took care of us the best he could and made sure we never wanted for anything. He taught me what strength is and how to face any problem with focus and determination.

Today, I realize that my grandfather's death was the first time in my life I honestly felt scared. Even though I'd experienced the turmoil of my parents' divorce and the move up North, I was too young to really understand what it would mean for my life. At fourteen years of age, I was old enough to feel every emotion tied to losing someone so important, and I sensed the uncertainty of what was to come.

CHAPTER 7

Big Lou

The LORD is good to all,
and his mercy is over all that he has made.

—Psalm 145:9 (ESV)

I think everyone in the house had the same fear of the unknown when my grandfather passed on, but, of course, no one spoke about it. That was my family; we kept our emotions locked safely inside (for better or worse). Even my grandmother, who surely must have had her own moments of deep pain after my grandfather's death, never let us see her down. She just kept on keeping on, and that meant continuing to go to work every day at the ceramic factory where she and most of the women in our family punched the clock for most of their adult lives.

I admired the brave face she put on after Papa's death. They'd been married more than forty years, so she not only lost her life partner, but also her soul mate and provider. She surely must have been devastated. Nonetheless, she tried her best to take over where Papa left off, particularly when it came to keeping us kids on the straight and narrow.

Unfortunately for my grandmother, Papa was the only great enforcer. We knew we couldn't tangle with him and win, but our petite grandmother was a different story; her bark was much stronger than her bite. There isn't a teenager alive who won't try to get away with as much as they can if given the chance; and my brother, sister, and I were no different. With only Mama there to snap the whip, we began to do more and more as we pleased.

First on that long list was skipping church. Every Sunday morning, before Mama could get dressed and ready for service, my brother, sister, and I would hightail it to a friend's house or hide in the basement of our house, or even in a closet—we'd hide anywhere we thought she wouldn't look and couldn't find us. She tried so hard to round us up. She'd call out to us, and even look around the house a bit, until she just got frustrated, threw up her hands, and went on her way, her perfectly matching hat and purse at her side.

As time went on, skipping church would be the least of my offenses. I began rebelling on every level and in every possible way I could think of. There were times I would run away from home for days at a time in a failed attempt to get away from the stifling eyes, suffocating rules, and rigid discipline of my grandmother. I'd be gone for maybe two or three days, until one of my uncles, usually Uncle Willie, would come and find me crashing at a friend's house. Good old Uncle Willie would lecture me something good on the way home, and then my grandmother would give me the evil eye for days, but I would do the exact same thing a couple of weeks later. I was insufferable.

Around this time, I also began hanging out more with my buddies and bumming a cigarette or a drink to pass the night away. I also decided that my presence was required quite regularly at all the infamous house parties in the area. If you've ever seen the African-American cult-classic film *Cooley High*, you have some idea how much trouble, fun, and damaging a house party can be. There was nothing like one back in those days, and I tried my best to get to every single one in my neighborhood.

The kids who hosted the parties at their house charged about twenty-five cents to get in and usually set the party up in their basement. Every home back then had a basement, where the kids could play or an unhappy husband could move to when things got too unpleasant upstairs. There'd be chips to munch on, some drinks, and then the "real" (alcoholic) drinks. We'd let loose, dancing all night to the good old music from those times, like the Temptations, Marvin Gaye, and the Supremes. Everyone wasn't dancing, of course. Some of my friends were in the corner, doing who knows what with God knows whom. I plead the Fifth on where I spent my time! Sometimes I'd go to these parties with my brother or sister, but by the end of the night, we'd all go our separate ways to do our own thing.

As I continued to sink further into my bad-girl ways, I decided to make use of my size in a less-than-positive way. Now, I didn't go looking for fights, but if someone wanted to start one, I was ready to go. My next-door neighbor, Geraldine Parham, was around my same age, and she was always in the mood to start something. She had what the kids today would call the most "stank" attitude and most certainly thought she was cuter than every other girl in the neighborhood. All she had to do was give me a sideways look or a dismissive hand gesture and it was on. On average, we probably fought once a week, and they weren't just little girlie scuffles either. Cuts and bruises were common, and yes, we loved to pull each other's hair out (okay, that was girlie, I know). To this day, I still have a few bald spots in the back of my head, all because of Geraldine.

That's also about the time that my alter ego, "Big Lou," was born. My smarty-pants sister Vivian started calling me that after I had one of my neighborhood brawls and won hands-down. I really earned my nickname during another memorable fight with a girl from another neighborhood. At a high school basketball game, this girl kept standing up during the game, making it impossible for anyone, especially me, to see. Man, was I salty. She was known as somewhat of a bully at school, so no one dared to ask her to sit down. Well, Big Lou did. I said in my kindest voice, "Could you please sit down so others can see?"

The girl turned around and looked at me with this nasty glance that screamed, *you and me—outside!* After the game, we did just that, but I was savvy enough to lure her to my neighborhood before we threw down, and she was dumb enough to follow. There was no way I was getting beaten up in my own neighborhood with so many friends and family around. Back then, it was all about neighborhood love, so we were always there for each other in a pinch. Just like James Brown said, "Papa don't take no mess," well, Big Lou didn't either. Many a girl in my neighborhood had to learn that the hard way.

I was sliding down a dangerous and slippery slope in my teen years, and again, no one in my family seemed to notice. Our mother surely would have if we'd been in constant contact. Though we remained close to her as the years went on, as teenagers we didn't make the trek to her home as often once we entered high school. Those were the days that I really regretted not living with our mother. It shouldn't have been a matter of having to make time to see our mother on the weekends. We should have been with her all the time. Without a doubt, this was a part of the anger I carried with me at all times. Why couldn't I have the life most children had, with a mother right where she was supposed to be? It would take years for me to realize and understand that God puts us exactly where he wants us to be, no matter how much we may disagree.

During our teen years, my brother fancied himself a singer and joined a singing group that sounded like the Temptations. I was in a similar kind of group known as the Supremes (not the *real* ones!). I have to admit my brother had a wonderful voice. He sang the lead in his group, while I sang background vocals in mine. My voice was pretty good but I never felt comfortable with the spotlight in any way. In fact, I ran from it and kept running from it until years later.

In reality, the singing groups were just another way to entertain ourselves. Back then, video games, TV on-demand, Facebook, and Twitter didn't exist, so we had to make our own fun, the old-fashioned way. We played jacks, kickball, and spent a lot of time at the school, entering talent shows and attending the evening parties. School was definitely the center of all things when I was younger.

Let me clarify: *activities* at school were the center of things—my schoolwork, not so much. I was too consumed with drinking, fighting, and staying away from church to focus on my books. I was doing just enough to get by in class, and that wasn't much. It wasn't that I didn't know the value of an education back then, because I did. I'd thought about attending college, but without financial assistance, and barely passing grades, college wasn't much more than a fleeting thought. I did know, however, that I did not want to end up working at the ceramic factory, like the other women in my family. That was a dead-end job, and I couldn't imagine anything worse than getting stuck like that.

There are times even today when I think about the choices we know we have, and the choices we have no idea we have when we are children. From early on in the lives of all my children and grand-children, I've made it clear that it was a must to get a higher educa-tion, and that meant working hard and doing well in school. No one in my life ever sat me down and had that talk with me when I was young. Part of the reason was that my own family didn't have a chance to go far in school (though a few of my mother's sisters did go to college), so I didn't see the chance of us doing it either. I was determined not to make that same mistake with my own children.

Though I didn't get the opportunity to pursue college until much later in my life, I'm a firm believer that parents have to let their children know what's expected of them so they have guide-lines and goals to focus on. I could have used a few of those guide-lines myself as I continued on my self-destructive path as a teen.

CHAPTER 8

School Daze

Those who sow in tears shall reap in joy.

—Psalm 126:5 (NKJV)

My height finally came in handy when I was chosen to play on the girl's high school basketball team at school. To my own surprise, I actually was pretty good at it. Finally my height was working for me and not against me, as it had for so many years. Maybe things were beginning to look up.

Not. Yes, there were good things that were beginning to happen in my life (like basketball), but other things remained the same. My situation at home was still unpleasant, and while I spoke to my mother often, it was difficult to get to see her as much as I would have liked. The anger and frustration I constantly lived with on the inside for years was still there, bubbling underneath with no way out, and like a boiling pot that had been left unattended, it threatened to overflow at any moment.

I certainly won't forget the day it finally did. Despite all of the dysfunction at home, I still was very close to my family. My cousins, sister, brother, and others were very important to me, and we protected each other from anyone or anything in the outside world that might cause us harm. Several of my cousins were my age, or close to it, and shared classes with me.

During those days, the schools were somewhat mixed, and we had teachers from all backgrounds and races. But this was still the '60s, and African Americans, even children, weren't getting the respect they deserved. Some of the nonblack teachers had little regard for us "little Negro children," and they didn't do much to hide their disdain.

One of those teachers was a white male math teacher, I don't recall his name, or maybe I just intentionally wiped it from my memory because it was too painful to hold on to. Either way, there is one encounter with him that still haunts my very being. This particular teacher was always yelling or referring to us in the most negative of tones. You could hear the disgust and scorn in his voice, and it stung us as young black children to feel that hate.

One day, he began lashing out at one of my cousins about her homework, bringing her close to tears. At that moment all I could see was red as the nasty words continued to roll off his tongue. Then I just snapped. Without thought or notice, I picked up a newly sharpened pencil from my desk and lunged toward the teacher, stabbing him with as much force as I could in his neck. What happened next is still pretty much a blur to me. I don't remember the teacher yelling out in pain or falling down to the floor. I do remember seeing blood, so I'm sure he needed medical attention. What I really remember vividly is what happened to me as a result.

I'd attacked a teacher, and not just any teacher, a white male teacher. I was facing charges as a juvenile, and the possibility of being put into a facility for years, away from my family and friends. If that same incident occurred today, I would have been put in jail with no questions asked. The rules are so much tougher, and no one gets a free pass. But God is so good, and even then, though I'd moved away from the church and its teachings, He was there for me, guiding my life and my future, and what a blessing that was, because my father's family had no idea what to do when this happened. These were hardworking, God-fearing people who didn't have run-ins with the law. They didn't know lawyers, or anyone well versed in the law, and they had no idea how to fight a legal system not known for supporting blacks.

My fate rested in the hands of the school board and the juvenile detention of the county jail. Wonders of wonders, both made the decision not to put me into a facility but to send me to another high school for a year. That was the extent of my punishment, and to this day I thank God for it. I don't think I could have survived being put in a detention center, away from the real world and my family. Still, as happy as I was with the relatively light sentence I received for the stabbing incident, I had no idea how difficult it would actually be for me long-term. I would now have to leave my neighborhood and friends to walk twelve miles across town to attend a new high school, a rival one at that. Is there anything worse than a rival high school? The distance meant I had to wake up before dawn to get to school on time, which also meant I didn't return home until late in the afternoon. My grandmother could have given me the fifty cents to ride the bus if she'd wanted to. She didn't. She wanted me to really feel the consequences of my actions. Just like that, my carefree, rebellious days were over. To add insult to injury, one of the additional requirements of my punishment was that I also needed to maintain good grades, something I'd been less than committed to before the incident.

But, as Dinah Washington so famously said, "What a difference a day makes."

With my new set of circumstances, I studied from the time I got home from school until I fell asleep at night. The year before that one, there wasn't a person around who could have convinced me I'd be doing that! And, not surprisingly, my family gave little support, mainly because my grandmother, father, and aunts felt I'd brought my troubles on myself, so I'd have to bear the brunt of the punishment alone. I guess in some ways they had a point. Even my mother, who was always in my corner, said little to me about the incident. It was clear she was not pleased, and it was also clear she'd make no effort to soften the blow.

I struggled to survive in a new school (with no friends) while dealing with the realization that I'd put myself in that situation. And I thought my young life had been lonely and empty before, but I had no idea what loneliness was until that fateful year. Amazingly, in the end I not only endured that year, but I actually grew up a little as a result. I learned a lot about myself during that time—after all, I had all the time in the world to do so on those long walks across town. I also realized that I could handle anything, no matter how difficult, disappointing, or heartbreaking. I felt the immense favor God had upon my life.

That period in my life is something I reflect on a great deal when I'm speaking to young girls and women of all ages about the importance of having a can-do attitude. I tell them that whatever they are going through at that moment, no matter how difficult, just give it to God. I'm a witness that He will work with you and do anything you ask Him to do for you, if you have the right attitude.

That year turned out to be the most difficult of my young life, but I knew it could have been so much worse. By the time my punishment was finished that year, my grades had improved twofold, and I was on my way back to my old neighborhood, my old school, and, I thought, my old life. But God had other plans.

CHAPTER 9

"He's So Fine"

Give thanks in all circumstances;
for this is the will of God in Christ Jesus for You.

—1 Thessalonians 5:18 (ESV)

Behold, children are a heritage from the LORD,
the fruit of the womb a reward. Like arrows in the hand
of the warrior are the children of one's youth.

—Psalm 127:3-4 (ESV)

M y return to Westside High was humbling, to say the least. Foolishly, I somehow thought time would stand still and things would be exactly as I left them in my old world. But, of course, time waits for no one; not even a wayward sixteen-year-old girl desperately trying to find herself.

To get back into the groove of things, I tried to become involved in activities that I found interesting before my year away. I became

Me at 16 years of age in 1970. Say it loud: "I'm black and I'm proud!"

one of the flag girls for the drill team. I'd always loved the way they looked, stepping out proudly before the games with flags for the country and the school. They seemed so fabulously chic. To my surprise, I was chosen immediately to become a member, and with that you couldn't tell me anything. Talk about a shot of confidence! I would float on cloud nine each time I put on my silky, white leotard, paired with green shorts underneath, and white patent leather boots with tassels. Yes indeed. I thought I was too cute, and I was! It was the first time I'd ever really appreciated what my height could do for me and that it was okay not only to be seen, but to be looked at as well.

In those days, we were never really told much about dating, relationships, and what to do or not do with the opposite sex. Boys were these fascinating mysteries we girls couldn't wait to discover. I do, however, recall my grandmother constantly telling me and my sister to "keep your dress tail down." Now, I had absolutely no idea what that meant, and it was clear that our grandmother had absolutely no intention of explaining it. I assumed she thought that at some point we'd figure it out for ourselves.

As is the case with all children and teenagers, being told what not to do without a logical explanation of why we weren't to do it was an open invitation to do wrong. As far as I knew, I had my dress tail up all the time! Of course, in reality what my grandmother was trying to say without actually saying it was not to become sexually active with young men. But that warning would fall on deaf years as I moved toward my senior year in high school.

Years later, I would be much more proactive with my own children, and even more so now with my grandchildren. I never hesitated to discuss male/female relationships, sex, and birth control with my sons and daughters. Even though my grandkids are still a little on the young side, I sometimes point out simple things, like how boys show they're interested in girls, and how to behave like ladies and gentlemen at all times. Information is key, and this generation is exposed to so much more than previous generations that we do ourselves and them a great disservice by not being up-front about issues these kids are sure to face in today's world.

I was just winging it during my teen years, not really sure where I was headed at a time when my future should have been its brightest. Though I'd learned a valuable lesson just the year before about actions and consequences, it didn't take long for me to resume a few of my other not-so-positive extracurricular activities. Drinking wine, beer, and smoking a little weed became more than a casual social occurrence during my last two years of high school. Though we were teenagers, it was beyond easy to get all the beer and wine we wanted. We'd just hang out outside the liquor store for a few hours and give someone the right age some money. It was as simple as that.

During those days, peer pressure was how the devil did his work in my life. I was so eager to belong and so desperate to fit in that I didn't think twice about going along with anything to get along with the crowd. I already looked different—so I was not about to act different too.

It didn't help that drinking heavily was something of a habit on my father's side of the family. My grandfather drank hard liquor to the point of having cirrhosis of the liver, and my father enjoyed his libations a little too much as well. It was how they let loose and relaxed after a hard week and during rough times. I would have to fight those same demons as I got older, but in high school, enjoying myself was all I had in mind.

Since money was a constant issue in our family and we had zero options for outside help, college wasn't in the cards for my siblings or me. So, like many young girls in high school back then, I hung out with friends after school, with the hope of eventually meeting a guy who would somehow change my life. Soon, through some friends I met "that guy." I was completely crazy for him, and boy, did he change my life. He was a few years older, and just so happened to be in college, which really made me feel like quite the grown-up.

In high school it always seemed that guys were intimidated by my height, so I didn't actually date very much up to this point. Joe Toney was my boyfriend's name, and the fact that this older college guy wanted to date little ole me just made my world spin. Even my no-nonsense grandmother seemed to like him (or showed no objection to him), and that was a miracle in itself.

Unfortunately, I was so blinded by my need for love and attention that I didn't pick up on some of the early warning signs that Joe was definitely not "the one." I certainly indulged in my share of vices, but to their detriment, many of my friends got in over their heads with drugs and drinking. That's what happened to Joe.

But, before the streets caught up with him, he was truly the stuff dreams were made of. He was about the same height as I was (6'2") and he was sort of handsome—but not in a "pretty boy" way. He had smooth, mocha skin; soft, curly hair; and an infectious grin that made my stomach quiver every time I saw him. And what a gentleman he was; he'd open doors for me, hold my hand, and he would share with me all that he had and more. I didn't know much about love at sixteen years old, but I had a feeling that what Joe and I had was somewhere in the ballpark.

It wasn't long before the two of us became completely inseparable. It didn't occur to my teenage mind to ask how he could be a college student and spend so much time with me every day. All I could think about was how good it felt to have a man who wanted to spend all of his free moments with me. I was absolutely in my own fantasy world for about a good year and a half, but a reality check was definitely on its way.

CHAPTER 10

"Tonight's the Night . . ."

Every child of God can defeat the world,
and our faith is what gives us this victory.

—1 John 5:4 (CEV)

My senior prom night in 1971 was such a magical time for me and my friends, and having my college boyfriend escort me to the dance made it all the better. My grandmother had taught me how to sew, and my skills had gotten so advanced in home economics (I was quite the class star) that I actually made my own prom dress. I spent weeks looking for just the right shoes and purse to match my master homemade creation.

The night itself was indeed amazing; it was everything any girl could have hoped for. Because prom night was a huge deal, my friends and I were given permission to stay out as late as we wanted, and we had every intention of doing just that. Since we had freedom we normally didn't have, Joe and I decided to take a very major step that night. We'd wanted to express our feelings for each other in a more tangible way for a while and decided we could best do that by spending the night together for the first time.

Now, this was a pretty serious step to take, especially given my family's intense religious beliefs and my mortal fear of my grandmother's wrath. But a little sweet talk, love, and just the right smile from a boy you're crazy about can make you do just about anything. It was earth-shattering.

In the weeks that followed our first time together, we'd see each other every day, and we became closer than ever. I felt like I was walking on air and the luckiest girl in the world to have such a connection with someone so special and who felt the same way. Then the nausea and morning sickness began, though I pretended not to notice. I was in complete denial about my condition. I just went about my business, finishing high school during the day and hanging out with friends at night. What else could I do?

That's exactly how I ended up on the couch that bright summer afternoon with my mother and grandmother demanding to know what was happening with me. Though being a pregnant teenage girl happened all the time back then (there were even a few other teenage expectant mothers on my block) just as it does today, it was still frowned upon, and—goodness gracious!—my grandmother was going to do some serious frowning on me. It would be a slap in the face to all the Christian values she'd taught me and that I had learned in church.

For this reason, I'm not sure why I was so stunned that day when my grandmother and mother approached me. Besides having that pregnancy glow, in those days parents and family members watched their children like eagles watch their young. They wanted to make sure there was nothing unacceptable going on and that no surprises were on the way. Anything your family missed, the neighbors picked up on. It might sound cliché, but it was truly a village back then, where everyone was connected and everyone cared. That's why I'm always amazed when I hear stories of children doing just about anything right under their parents' noses these days. Young girls being eight months pregnant without anyone noticing or boys building bombs in the family basement that wind up killing their classmates—that kind of thing really bewilders me. How do you not know what's going on in your own house? My grandparents and aunts noticed everything we did and had no problems confronting us if they thought something wasn't right.

Ironically and thankfully, as I got older my grandmother began to reach out more to my mother. She really had to when my siblings or I started to get out of hand. She knew confronting me or any of us alone would probably be very unpleasant; but having our mother come down from her home would keep everyone calm, cool, and collected.

My mother was the loving woman she always was that day she found out about Shaquille. She may have been a little disappointed, but she let me know she still loved me and would be there for me no matter what. That was my mother, kind and loving to a fault. You never had to worry that she wouldn't listen to everything you had to say or give you a fair chance. My grandmother was quite a different story. The criticisms and negative comments that came my way via her and my father's family were disheartening, degrading, and demoralizing, to say the least! I was made to feel as though I'd committed the worst crime known to man. I wanted to die.

I may not have known it then, but the Lord was indeed watching over me when I needed Him the most. Yes, I knew I'd made a mistake, but what could I do about it at that point? Abortion was out of the question, and besides, I wanted to keep my baby. If anyone in my household had really taken the time to understand, they may have realized that my need for love was why I was having a baby in the first place. At seventeen, I was old enough to know the consequences of having unprotected sex, and I chose to do it anyway. Now, I'm not sure I fully understood that may have been the reason I was pregnant at seventeen, but then again, I didn't understand much back then. I knew that I had to accept the fact that I was going to be a mother. I was ready and willing to do whatever it took to be a good one.

As if there weren't enough unhappy people in my life, the baby's father, Joe, was really not pleased about my pregnancy. He let me know in no uncertain terms that he did not want to be a father at that time and wouldn't be contributing much to our baby's future. Again, I was crushed. That's when I began to see clearly some of the things I had turned a blind eye to for a long time.

Joe had a substance abuse problem that was disrupting his life, and now it was also disrupting my life and the life of our baby. Words can't accurately describe how devastatingly heartbreaking it was for me to see the man I loved fall prey to addiction. All too many good men and women back then, as they do now, became addicted to drugs, not only ruining their lives but also shattering the lives and dreams of the many people who loved them the most.

Joe and I continued to date a little while longer after I told him the news, but things just weren't the same. In a different time and place, I would have proven my love and tried to help Joe kick his habit and get back on track, but I had a baby on the way, and that was going to take all of me. I gradually phased Joe out of my life—not because I wanted to, but because I had to. That I had to push him out of my life at all is something that still upsets me, and back then, I blamed the world and everyone else I could for it.

CHAPTER 11

The Little Warrior

*Believe in the Lord Jesus, and you will be saved—you and
your household.*

—Acts 16:31

Believe it when I say I'm not someone who usually blames my
problems on others, but Joe's plunge into drugs was more than
his own doing. The ugly face of racism, coupled with the backdrop
of the Vietnam War and the recent deaths of Martin Luther King
Jr. and Bobby Kennedy, made it easy for a young African-American
man to become hopeless and turn to drugs. This, in turn, made it
even easier for him to just walk away from his child and me.

In just a matter of weeks, my world had turned upside down and
my life had changed drastically. Because of the reactions from my
grandmother and other family members, I completely withdrew
from everyone after I graduated from high school. I attended my
final classes and came right back home afterward, speaking as little

as I could to anyone for any reason. I was angry at my family and at myself at this point. Not only was the man I loved no longer available to me, but also now the people who were supposed to love me proved to be just as distant.

My personal funk didn't (or couldn't) last very long. I soon realized that wallowing in self-pity wouldn't do my unborn baby or me much good. So I picked myself up and went about the business of getting my life together. I had a high school diploma, so that would have to count for something. In the '70s, before Reagan got in the White House and axed most of the public assistance given to the poor, the government offered pretty extensive support and programs for low-income, single mothers. I decided to make the most of it. I filled out what seemed to be an endless amount of forms and answered all their questions at social services before getting to see the doctors I needed for prenatal care.

That was the longest nine months of my life. I cried all the time—most times for no reason and other times when I thought of what the future actually held for me and the new life growing inside me.

Still, despite the turmoil and my own anxiety, my oldest child, Shaquille, was born with relative ease at 8 a.m. on Wednesday, March 6, 1972. Most people are amazed when I tell them that my now seven-foot-one, three-hundred-plus-pound son weighed a measly seven pounds when he was born. (My oldest daughter weighed eight pounds at birth.) Therefore I had no warning (though my own height provided a clue) that he'd become the massive force he is today. The only thing I knew for sure from the moment the nurse brought my baby to me in the hospital that day was that he had the smoothest brown skin, the most pensive eyes, and sweetest smile—he captured my heart from the start.

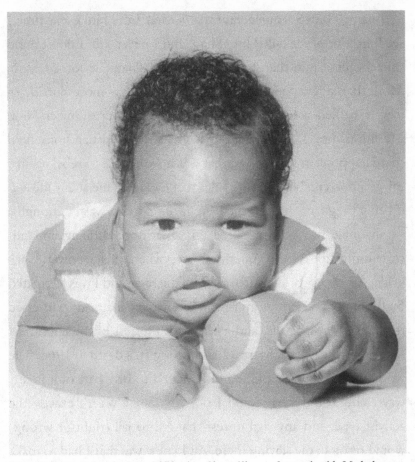

This photo was taken in June 1972 when Shaquille was 3 months old. My baby was born to be an athlete.

I will always believe that the tough circumstances surrounding his birth are just one of the many reasons Shaquille and I have always had a special bond. Now, that's not to say that I don't share a special bond with all four of my children, because I most certainly do. But as mothers, we often interact differently with each child depending on their needs, personalities, and circumstances. My relationship with my oldest son remains strong to this day, and I know I'm truly blessed to have it.

I named him Shaquille, and that's what I call him every time I see him. I've never called him Shaq, and I never will. I don't mind others calling him that, but I named him Shaquille for a reason. More than a few people in my family and a few more outside of it were baffled as to why I decided to give all four of my children Muslim names. I'd grown up in such a strict Christian household that I suppose, in some ways, that was how I chose to rebel against my grandparents' suffocating rules that had irked me all my life—as if being pregnant without the benefit of marriage wasn't enough.

Shaquille was born in 1972, an all-at-once thrilling and un-certain time for African Americans everywhere. Black power, black pride, African garb, and Afros were all the rage, and I was fascinated by the unity and optimism of the moment. I'd already witnessed the 1967 Newark riots, and along with the rest of the country, I felt deeply the pain of Martin Luther King Jr.'s death in 1968. The world was changing rapidly, and I wanted to be a part of it in any way I could. But what could I do? My family wasn't exactly the activist type, and any civil unrest that led to jail (right or wrong) would result in me staying there. All I knew was that I had to make my mark somehow.

Divine intervention sometimes comes in the most unexpected ways. A few years before I became pregnant with Shaquille, an Islamic mosque was built in our neighborhood, no doubt a result of the popularity of the Nation of Islam and Malcolm X. I caught headlines here and there about the Muslim movement, but for the most part, I never fully appreciated what they were doing or what they stood for. In our house, politics were rarely discussed, and when they were, we as children were not included in the conversa-tion. The old adage that children were to be seen and not heard was in full effect in my house, which made the Black Muslim platform seem ions away from my little block in New Jersey.

Maybe it was that lack of knowledge that had me so fascinated with the mosque and what it represented in our neighborhood. Its teachings were the polar opposite of all I'd learned as a child, and that was right up my alley. Some days I'd go into the mosque's gift store in the mornings and wander the book aisles for hours, looking for anything that caught my eye. One book that did catch my eye was a collection of Islamic names and their meanings. This was the period when blacks were actually giving their children names that stood for something, and I decided this could be my way of making a statement—giving my firstborn child a name that spoke to the times in which we were living.

The name Shaquille stuck in my mind immediately because it meant "little one," and the middle name I gave him, Rashaun, meant "warrior." I liked the idea of my son being a warrior in a world that could be pretty harsh, particularly toward African Americans. Since his father had abandoned his parental responsibilities, my firstborn and I were both going to have to be true warriors together in order to survive.

CHAPTER 12

Why They Do It

[God] will yet fill your mouth with laughter
and your lips with shouts of joy.

—Job 8:21

The first few months after Shaquille's birth were probably the toughest for me. I still felt the blues on some level, and no one thought enough of me to explain that it was the result of my hormones being out of whack. It didn't help that I had absolutely no idea what to do with a newborn baby, and my grandmother let me know that every chance she got. But I was determined to learn as much as I could as fast as I could, because my baby was depending on it. What's ironic is how all the ridicule and chastising I received before Shaquille's birth miraculously disappeared once he was born. My grandmother couldn't get enough of my baby, and quite frankly treated him like he was her own; but I stood my ground. I was his mother, and as easy as it would have been to just allow my grandmother to raise my child so I could go out and do my own thing—I couldn't do it. I wouldn't do it.

If she was holding him, I'd be sitting right next to her, waiting for her to put him down. I never left his side. I often think our children know when we've fought and sacrificed for them above and beyond what's normal, even if we've never told them. I feel there's a part of Shaquille that knows I was always there for him, even though I was just a child myself. That's the unique connection we share, and so far it's been unbreakable.

When Shaquille was a few months old, I got a job through a government program that assisted single mothers. I would leave my baby with the babysitter during the day, then come home and focus all my attention on him. Occasionally, I would go out after work to socialize with other coworkers, but not very often. I had a responsibility to be a mother to my child, and I planned on fulfilling it. It was incredibly important for me to get out and go to work after Shaquille's birth and get off of public assistance for several reasons. First, I wanted to feel like I could do something on my own and do it well. I'd never had a crutch to lean on, and I didn't want depending on one to become a habit. Also, I wanted to continue the legacy of my own family's work ethic.

Today, I often talk to young girls who are single mothers, and I encourage them to do what I did and go to work; working gave me that sense of self that I'd been longing for and still need. It can be all too easy to lose yourself and become overwhelmed when you become a mother so young. It's easy to fall into a world of self-pity and worthlessness when your plan, or your option to have a plan, goes off track. God knows I was depressed in the months before my baby's birth, and sometimes afterward. Postpartum depression wasn't even a term discussed back then, so I have no idea if that was what I was suffering from. I just figured I had the blues because of all of the huge changes happening so rapidly in my life.

Of course, I realize that my teenage pregnancy was nearly thirty-eight years ago, when being a single mother still had a very negative stigma attached to it. I sometimes wish it had more of a negative stigma today. I meet so many young ladies who are in their teens with two or three children, and my heart hurts for all of them. Talk about mental welfare. With so much information available today, I often get confused as to why these young girls don't take more control over their lives.

But I also understand that wanting unconditional love from someone is as strong an urge now as it was when I was a young girl. Having a child gives you that unconditional love without question, and that's something we all crave. Unfortunately, just as I didn't, most girls don't realize how difficult being a child while raising a child can be. I don't think it's lost on anyone that many of our young girls today also suffer from very low self-esteem. When you combine low self-esteem with the lack of hope for a bright future, you have some powerful deterrents to avoiding a pregnancy.

As tough as it was for young African Americans in the late '60s and '70s, I sometimes think it's even more difficult now to be a young adult. Today's children are forced to grow up before their time and are exposed to images and sights way beyond their understanding. We live in a time when society teaches our children that they should have it all right now, without providing them the tools to acquire it through hard work. If I'd had those same influences as a child, I'm not sure how I would have turned out. Something told me then, and the Spirit tells me now, that neither I nor any of my children would have the life we have now if I hadn't made the decision to step out on faith and make my own life better.

CHAPTER 13

"That's the Way Love Goes"

Let the husband render to his wife the affection due her,

and likewise also the wife to her husband.

—1 Corinthians 7:3 (NKJV)

Once I became comfortably settled into my new life with my new baby and my new job, I tried my best to maintain a strict schedule. I went straight to work and came right back home. That wasn't exactly the active social life of the average eighteen-year-old, but I felt so much like an adult with a child waiting at home for me that I wanted to make sure my actions said just that.

My days of house parties and nights out with friends were officially over, though I did manage to find my way back to my favorite alcoholic beverage from time to time. For the most part, my life revolved around work and my son. It was quite a challenge, and trust me, it was more than enough to deal with. Still, there were moments when I couldn't help longing for a little more.

Me and Shaquille in August 1972. "Mommy, stop tickling me!"

While my new schedule kept me busy and on the go, I still thought occasionally about the path not taken and how things might have been different for me if I'd had the money for college and had been able to actually follow my dreams of becoming a public speaker. I'm sure these are typical thoughts for anyone whose life had been as drastically altered as mine had been. But I loved to fantasize about seeing the world, even if I had no idea where to start or how I'd get there.

Of course, those fleeting thoughts of traveling to far-off places and going to college had to be put on the back burner as I focused on the life I actually did have. Thankfully, and somewhat surprisingly, my grandmother allowed me to keep the money I made from working for the city to buy things for my baby and me. I'd chip in cash for food, but I didn't have to pay for rent or utilities, which left me in pretty good shape each month.

Since I was only eighteen years old and still very fixated on fashion, I'd take that extra money and buy the sharpest clothes I could find for Shaquille and me. I enjoyed nothing more than playing with and dressing my baby up every day. My grandmother would often have to remind me that Shaquille wasn't a toy. She'd pass my room in the mornings while I was getting my son ready and snap loudly, "That ain't no doll." She'd say that because I was constantly brushing his curly hair so he'd have parts on different sides of his head, never considering that a baby's head is much too tender to constantly brush. Lord, I just know my baby probably had a headache all the time! Still, he never cried as I completed his elaborate grooming routine. After I'd comb his hair, I'd "grease" him up and down with Vaseline so his skin would be smooth, soft, and shiny. Then I'd put plenty of baby powder all over him so he would always smell fresh and clean. Is there anything better than a sweet-smelling baby? Finally, I'd dress him in the cutest clothes I could find at Macy's or any other local department store near where we lived. My son had to look sharp as a tack at all times. Those were the good old '70s, and the fashions were fabulous and funky; bell-bottom pants, big collars, and loud colors were the outfits of choice.

I really loved to dress Shaquille in those cute little suede-patched sweaters and shorts with white socks when he was a toddler. He'd look so adorable until he got outside the house and headed straight for the mud puddles. Still, it felt good being able to buy my son all those things, because for some reason, and quite possibly because I'd proven that I was able to take care of myself and my baby (at least to some extent), my confidence had grown slightly in the previous months. I even began to like myself more when I put on my bright polyester and chiffon outfits that laid perfectly on my lean frame and long legs. I was wearing my hair in a short-cropped Afro during that time, and with my height topping off at 6'2", there was no convincing me that I didn't look good—real good!

Phillip Harrison must have agreed. Phillip was a very smooth and suave parks and recreation worker who came in weekly to pick up his paycheck from my office. Sometimes he'd come in twice a week to see if a new check had come in, which was sort of odd, but I paid it no mind. Each time he saw me, he'd always have a smile on his face and a kind word to offer. I thought he was nice, but I didn't give him much more thought after that. Now, had I been a little quicker in my cognitive skills, I would have picked up on the signals that this man was interested in me. But my mind had totally been in mommy mode for that last year or so, which meant the finer points of dating weren't exactly fresh on my brain.

Eventually, there was no denying that a mutual attraction was brewing between us, and finally Phillip asked me out on our first date. I was so impressed by him and how worldly he seemed. He was nearly six years older than me, had traveled to different places around the country, and had seen and done things I could only imagine. What can I say? I was smitten.

In addition to his many charms, Phillip, or Phil, as I began to call him, was also quite the romantic. He was constantly showering me with compliments and sending flowers and cards to my office and home. To once again have an older man interested in me (notice a pattern here) made me feel not only like a very special young lady, but also like a woman who was ready to live a true adult life with a "real" man.

In retrospect, the habit I had of being attracted to older men spoke volumes about where I was as a young woman. Though it didn't occur to me then, and as cliché as it may sound now, I believe that I was searching for the father figure I never really had as a young girl. My father was never a very involved presence in my life because of his handicap. Papa had been a strong male influence, but a grandfather and a father have two very different roles in a young girl's world. I guess on some level, and at some point in our lives, all women long for the comfort of finding security with a man they trust and love. Our fathers are usually the first men in our immediate surroundings who provide us with those two things. But if we don't have that father in our lives, as far too many African-American women don't, we're left with this huge void that we can go our entire adult life trying to fill. That's where I was when I met Phil. It wasn't a very healthy place for me to be, but the problem was I had no idea I even had a problem. Isn't that the case for many of us at one point or another in our lives?

Initially, my dates with Phil were quite simple—dinner here and there and maybe a movie. As much as I wanted a man in my life, I was also careful not to move too quickly, given my circumstances. After all, I was a new mother trying to get my life together. But on the other hand, I very much wanted a father figure in Shaquille's life sooner rather than later. He needed someone who could show him how to be strong, responsible, and confident. In essence, I wanted someone to show him how to be a man.

Let me be clear: I know there are many single mothers out there today doing the best they can to raise sons by themselves, and I applaud them; I really do. I know how difficult it is to be a mother when you have support, so I really take my hat off to women who do it alone. But I've always believed that only a man can truly teach a boy how to become a man himself.

Though he was only a little over a year old at the time, Shaquille was living in a house full of women who all adored him and who, quite frankly, spoiled him to no end. This was particularly the case with my grandmother, who thought he was the sun, the moon, and the stars. I wanted a man in my life who wanted to help raise my son and who would love him as much as I did. So I started to spend part of my dates with Phillip watching his demeanor and temperament. I watched him carefully to see how he handled the news that he'd be acquiring an instant family if our courtship were to proceed to the next level. He passed with flying colors.

Convincing Shaquille that *he* actually needed a father figure, now, that was another story.

CHAPTER 14

Daddy's Home!

My father and my mother have forsaken me,

but the LORD will take me [in].

—Psalm 27:10 (NASB)

Shaquille was used to having my undivided attention at all times, and after I met Phil, the thought of someone taking even a little bit of that away caused my little son to have more than a few hissy fits. Thankfully, Phil was determined to bond with my son no matter what and often planned outings for just the three of us. Needless to say, I was really falling in love with this man.

After he planned and took me to New York City for a wonderful weekend to tour the big city and take in a show, I knew he was the right one for me. It had only been five months, but I thought, *Why second-guess something I feel so strongly about?*

We married in a small ceremony at Phil's parents' home. Only a few family members and friends from work were in attendance. I wore a long, pink, dashiki-looking dress that I made myself, with a matching head wrap made from pink wedding-veil material. Picture this if you will: in an effort to have coordinating outfits, Phil wore a cranberry dashiki suit. After we took our vows, I danced to express my joy, while friends and family threw money at my feet. It wasn't exactly your typical wedding ceremony, but it was fabulous just the same. We had no money for a real honeymoon, so we spent the next few nights in his parents' attic apartment, having our own private "honeymoon."

Once we were thrust back into reality, Phil and I moved into the house that I shared with my grandmother and other family members. That house on Littleton Street never had a dull moment. What a way to kick off a marriage!

By the time we were actually married, Shaquille was about two years old, and he had perfected the "terrible twos." For better or worse, Phil was determined to help him learn how to behave. My new husband would realize the hard way that doing so was going to be a lot more difficult than it seemed.

Phil received a crash course one day when Shaquille wet his pants at day care. Phil and I both decided he needed to be taught a lesson. My son knew better than to wet himself, but this was his act of rebellion, even as a toddler.

Even if I try, I'm not sure I will ever be able to forget the scene at our house that day. Shaquille was in my grandmother's lap, and Phil motioned for her to put him down. My grandmother didn't (or wouldn't), and Shaquille didn't dare budge because he knew what was in store for him. So Phil, being the focused and determined man he was, reached in to take Shaquille out of my grandmother's lap. Bad move. My grandmother was just as focused and determined as Phil, and she wasn't about to let anyone take her grandson away. So, just as Phil reached for Shaquille, my grandmother pulled off her shoe and threw it directly at Phil's head. She hit her target like a bulls-eye, leaving a knot in the center of his forehead. Now, while my son thought it was the funniest thing that he'd ever seen, I knew an expiration date had just been placed on our living quarters.

My entire family blamed Phil for what had happened and began treating him accordingly, so to give things a chance to cool down after that incident, we moved in with his family on the other side of Newark. We stayed there for a few weeks, and I can't say I enjoyed that very much; but being married meant making compromises, so I tried to grin and bear it for as long as I could. I got along okay with his family, but we just truly needed our own space.

A funny side note is that some twenty years later, Shaquille and Phil would present my grandmother with that very shoe, bronzed, for her eighty-third birthday. She was blown away by the gift, and everyone in attendance knew about the shoe-throwing incident. She didn't need the infamous George Bush shoe-throwing incident for inspiration. She was ahead of her time.

During those days it was tough for us as a young couple; though we both made okay money in our respective jobs, it wasn't enough to find a decent place to live. Phil was a hard worker and wanted desperately to take care of his new family. I contributed money from my job, but it still wasn't enough to make ends meet. Something was going to have to change, and soon.

CHAPTER 15

Losing Lucille

We love because he first loved us.

—1 John 4:19

Married life takes a while to get accustomed to, especially if you're a nineteen-year-old girl who never really witnessed a healthy relationship up close and personal. And by healthy, I mean a relationship based on two equals working together toward the same goals. My grandparents, aunts, and uncles all had old-fashioned partnerships that flourished based on old-school thinking and rules.

As Phil and I continued to get to know each other and blend parenthood into our union, we were faced with the pressing issue of how we'd succeed financially in such trying times. Though the '70s offered a brand-new world of freedom and opportunities for African Americans, jobs were still hard to come by. Especially good jobs, the ones that offered adequate benefits, reasonable hours, and pay sufficient to take care of a growing family.

After a few months of looking in vain for a better job, Phil decided to join the Army. This was an attractive option for many African Americans during those times. The military offered training, housing, travel, and a chance to reach that elusive higher income so many of us were in search of. The timing was also just right because the Vietnam War had ended, and we were at peace. I cosigned on his decision, eager to finally have a home of our own and excited about the possibility of seeing the world outside of New Jersey. No one in my family had actually had the chance to travel around the country, much less the world, so I was jazzed about being the first one to do so.

We'd been married only about two months when Phil was whisked away to basic training in South Carolina. Shaquille and I once again stayed with my grandmother while Phil spent six weeks learning his new job in the military. Those weeks apart were torture for us, and to try to compensate, we'd speak on the phone daily for what seemed like hours at a time. Of course, long phone conversations meant high phone bills, and it wasn't long before my grandmother's phone was turned off due to nonpayment. My grandmother was so angry that once she had it turned back on (in my sister Vivian's name, mind you), I wasn't allowed to go near it. That's when Phil and I perfected our writing skills to stay in touch.

I must admit, Phil wrote me some passionate, lovely, and touching letters back then that helped pass the time.

My husband had to work up to a certain rank before we were assigned a place to stay, so it would be another year and a half before we actually received housing on the base. As luck would have it, we were initially stationed at Fort Monmouth in South Jersey, Eatontown, far enough from home to have our own lives but close enough to still have the support our families. We lived in a quaint little townhouse that we decorated with furniture from the military warehouse because that was all we could afford. Furniture from a military warehouse looked like a large office with beds. But it was home—our home—and it was more than we'd ever had before.

As we became settled into military life, Phil and Shaquille's relationship began to thrive as well, I think in part because I stepped back and just let it happen naturally. I didn't interfere or try to coddle my son. I knew Phil's no-nonsense but loving approach was the best for Shaquille's development in the long run, and that was the most important thing to me as a mother.

Though we'd moved a distance away, I continued to work in Newark. Even with Phil entering the military, the money he made still wasn't enough to live worry free. We had good benefits, like health care and housing, but we were still pinching pennies to stay afloat. The almost two-hour commute back and forth from the base to Newark was particularly hard on Shaquille and me. That's not to say that my son didn't just love our bus rides every day. He would stand up in his seat and press his little face to the window, squealing with glee as we passed cars, trees, and department stores. He was just a child at that point and had no idea how different he actually was or would be as time went on. Neither did I. At four years old, Shaquille was more than a head taller than most kids his age, and I was forced to carry his birth certificate with me at all times to avoid having fistfights with the train conductor or the bus driver about whether or not he should ride for free. I even had to show his birth certificate at McDonald's so he could get a Happy Meal!!

It was happening all over again, I thought, but this time to my child. I'd suffered the same types of stares and rejections because of my height, and it broke my heart that now my son would have to face the same thing, and much earlier in his life than I had. As parents, we try to do anything we can to prevent our children from suffering any injustice or pain, only to eventually realize it's rarely possible to provide them with complete protection. I would have to learn that lesson again with each one of my children.

CHAPTER 16

"Lean on Me"

Blessed are all those who put their trust in Him.

—Psalm 2:12 (NKJV)

Shaquille and I continued that long commute for another two years, until two weeks before I gave birth to my daughter Lateefah, who was born one pound heavier than her older brother. I'd suffered a miscarriage the year before, but the doctor assured us we would have no problem having more children. Thankfully, he was right.

As she'd been for most of my life, my mother was such a godsend during that time. She visited us regularly in order to help me with my growing brood. It was also a blessing that Shaquille was old enough not to be underfoot. He was six years old by then and quite able to get dressed on his own, keep himself entertained, and help out a little around the house. He'd been an only child for so long that I had no idea how he'd handle a new sibling in the house.

Six years seemed like a lifetime, particularly since my other children were born ten months apart. While it was just him, I think I gave my oldest son all the attention and focus he could handle. In turn, he was secure enough in our love that he showed no jealously or animosity toward his new sibling. In fact, he seemed to love the idea of being a big brother, something he still takes seriously to this day. There's nothing he wouldn't do for his brother and sisters, and vice versa.

Shaquille's pleasant attitude would surely come in handy when, less than a year later, I became pregnant again with my second daughter, Ayesha. My pregnancy with her proved to be much more emotionally straining on the entire family since she was born prematurely and had to stay in the hospital for three months due to the nondevelopment of her lungs. Trust me when I say that nothing is more heartbreaking or nerve-racking than having a sick child you can do nothing for. I felt so helpless with my baby away from me, and there were many days that I just wanted to completely break down. But I'd remember my other two babies at home, waiting for me to come take care of them too. Still, I'd spend hours on end at the hospital each day, listening to the doctors tell me my baby probably wouldn't survive. But she did survive, and to this day we call her our miracle baby.

Phil, who had been overseas working, came home and helped out in whatever ways he could, particularly with the children. He loved his kids and tried to do as much as he could with them after work. Ayesha's illness really strengthened our marriage. For a time, it brought us together in more ways than one. It wasn't long before I was pregnant again with my next son, Jamal. Now, picture this—Ayesha wasn't a year old. Lateefah was just about to turn two, and Shaquille was just turning eight. Talk about a full house!

Shaquille sitting on my lap in Grandma Odessa's kitchen in Jersey City, in the summer of 1978. It doesn't matter how big he gets, he will always be my baby boy!

But all the work also wore me out a bit. One night in particular stands out in my mind, and it was when Phil was on one of his frequent out-of-town training sessions. I was about seven months pregnant with Ayesha, Lateefah was not yet a year old, and Shaquille was seven at the time. We were driving home from somewhere in our little piece of a car when it suddenly started zigzagging all across the road. I pulled over to find that the front tire was flat. Now, even if I'd known how, I couldn't have changed the tire in my condition—and I didn't know how. We were on a dark, unlit road with very few cars passing by. What was I going to do? This was well before the convenience of modern inventions like cell phones and beepers that keep us all connected today. I don't know how we survived without them in those days. I was scared to death to be on the side of the road with two small children and a flat tire. I was so upset at that moment that I just sat down on the curb and cried. That wasn't the best move in front of the kids, but I truly didn't know what else to do.

Fewer and fewer cars were coming by. As I sat with my head down, sobbing, Shaquille got out of the car and came and sat down next to me. He put his hand on my shoulder and said "Mommy, don't cry. It will be okay." Just then, a car came down the road and immediately pulled over behind our car. The man got out, surveyed the damage, and changed the tire without saying a word. I was so overwhelmed with gratefulness, I still had tears in my eyes. I didn't even have a dollar to offer him, so I just gave him my hand as my show of thanks. Talk about an angel on the highway! I also remember that night well because it reminds me that even when Shaquille was very young, we still always had the emotional connection of support for each other.

When I told my mother about those types of incidents when we spoke during our weekly conversations, I think she could see that I was growing overwhelmed with all my added responsibilities. Her response was to begin regularly quoting Scriptures to me in an effort to lift my mood. Now, I loved my mother immensely, but the words she'd read from the Bible would often just go in one ear and out the other. I still had my biblical foundation, but I felt I'd somehow lost my connection to God. What a lonely place that was. It seemed like I'd fallen into a dark hole that was so deep and dank that I just kept sinking deeper and deeper with no way out.

In many ways, it was a hole I'd dug myself. In my mind, being a wife meant being the very best wife—*with no exceptions.* So I spent all my days making sure the house was spotless inside and out, that dinner was always ready on time, and that the children were clean and tidy before bedtime. Being a mother also meant being the best mother. I wanted to please my husband and my children in every way possible and did whatever it took to make it happen. I was confident I knew how to be the perfect mother and the perfect wife, but I had no idea how to be Lucille, whoever she was. I still hadn't taken the time to find out, and I really didn't have the time to.

Any woman can relate to the toll the desire to be perfect can put on you both physically and mentally. Back then, there was no such thing as a spa day or a girls' lunch to relax and recharge your spirits. I would relax my own hair with a perm solution from SoftSheen, paint and cut my own nails, and my facials consisted of me smearing Ivory soap and good old Vaseline on my face before I went to bed. So much for real pampering.

As my responsibilities grew, I slowly began to revert back to some of my past bad habits, and as time went on, I started drinking more heavily. Without a doubt, alcohol was the social activity of choice for enlisted people in the military.

The entire military culture is unique and one that is difficult to explain if you've never actually been a part of it. The military is like its own world, and the person who is actually in the service has the responsibility of making sure his family is on point at all times. Any misstep is a reflection of the enlisted person. I often joked with friends that when Phil enlisted, so did I.

While we lived on the base for the most part during this time, there were months when we lived in the city of New Jersey in an apartment, which caused even more worry for me as a mother. The streets of New Jersey were hard-core, with drug dealers, pimps, and other misfits hanging around at all times. Shaquille was about eight or nine years old, the perfect age for some of the criminals to put the wrong ideas in his head. The shine on a drug dealer can be pretty bright. He has the finest car, the best-looking jewelry, and the nicest home on the block.

For a struggling family like ours, Shaquille would have been any drug dealer's perfect recruit. He looked older than his age and had the most outgoing personality even then. So outgoing was his personality that he was always getting in trouble at school for being the class clown. More than a few times, Phil would make unscheduled visits to the classroom to surprise Shaquille and catch him in the act. Both of us often lectured him about his behavior and told him it was either going to get him a career in Hollywood or land him in serious trouble! Yes, we were trying to scare him. I loved his personality—he was always a ham, even in the crib, but I wasn't going to let him lose his way. I don't think it's a secret that when young African-American boys are considered class disrupters, it can permanently impact their futures. Teachers don't take them as seriously and therefore don't focus on their progress. Often, they wind up in special education classes or receive constant detention. Phil and I had to make Shaquille understand how important school was to his future. As a mother, I had to take control of the situation and not allow the streets or anything else to ruin my home.

Whenever I talk to parents today and they ask how I raised four well-adjusted kids, I tell them point-blank: by being aware of everything they did at all times. I made sure Shaquille was always busy after he returned from school. I didn't let him hang outside or spend a lot of time with the neighborhood boys. He was to do his homework and then attend several after-school programs we'd enrolled him in. This was also before Reagan was able to cut the majority of social after-school programs that really benefited inner-city communities. When I look at the crime rate and the death rates of young black teens today, it really hurts my heart. I believe that if those children had other productive activities, interests, and things to focus on, violence wouldn't be their only outlet. But parents can't be with their children twenty-four hours a day, and those social programs were a godsend for poor parents and their children. I thank God my children had options.

As Shaquille became older, I began to question how I'd bring up the subject of his birth father, Joe Toney. I'd debated for years on whether to tell my son about his real father and what, exactly, I'd say when I did. Shaquille wasn't in need of a father figure; he and Phil had bonded so well. But my sister lived near the home where Joe was staying with his mother, and I didn't want Shaquille to hear about his real father from someone else. So I summoned up my nerve and decided to sit my son down and tell him the truth about his father. I was all at once scared and profusely proud of myself reaching that point because I had no idea how he'd take it. In the simplest language I could think of, I laid out what happened before his birth (well, as much as I felt a child his age would understand), and why his father and I weren't together. Later that day, I took him to the Toney house and introduced him to his father and grandmother. It was a bit strained after the introductions, and in all honesty, I'm not sure Shaquille even understood what was happening. In his mind he already had a father; therefore the man he was meeting that day was just another face in the crowd. Still, I was proud of myself for being strong enough to deal with the subject head-on.

I always wanted to be honest with my children about everything I'd done in my life—the good, the bad, and the ugly. My mistakes and my successful moments. As parents, we must be honest and up front with our children if we expect them to do the same.

On a side note, Shaquille hasn't spoken to his birth father since that day.

CHAPTER 17

"Inner City Blues"

Be strong and take heart, all you who hope in the LORD.

—Psalm 31:24

As history will surely tell, Phil introduced Shaquille to basketball at around age five, so he played frequently on base or at the Boys and Girls Club in the community. I truly believe an idle mind is the devil's workshop, so I made sure Shaquille was involved in quality activities. I had to be committed as a mother to make sure my son stayed on the straight path and didn't allow others to stop him from having the life he wanted. Again, I'm confused when parents don't realize how important it is to know everything their child is and isn't doing. That's what real parenting is.

Still, I couldn't worry 24/7 about everything. Phil and I would try to let loose and have a good time whenever we could. With four kids and only one person working, money was tighter than ever. Our usual meals consisted of beans and franks, corned beef hash with grits on the side, or a sixty-nine-cent can of culinary delight known as "chicken à la king" over toasted bread. Boy, did the children hate when I made that every week. But it was cheap, fast, and it was enough to feed all of us with relative ease.

Since going out on actual dates that required money was out of the question, Phil and I would have other couples over for a game of spades or bid whist, and we'd all just drink the night away. Surprise, surprise, waking up early for church on Sunday morning was a no go because we were way too hung over to even get up before noon. Our little weekly ritual also helped squash our religious differences. I wasn't a practicing Christian, and Phil wasn't a practicing Muslim, so together we just didn't practice religion at all on Sunday!

But the semi-good times wouldn't last long. Shortly after the birth of Jamal, we were transferred to Fort Stewart in Hinesville, Georgia. We were now living in the very deep South, a huge departure from New Jersey. The South had its own slow way of life, and it took some getting used to for all of us. We were also still struggling financially with four mouths to feed. Struggling so bad, we had to go on public assistance. Phil and I hated to do that, but we had to feed our children somehow, so we applied for food stamps. I'd asked for help before Shaquille was born, but I despised that helpless feeling. Nonetheless, if you do need help, there's no shame in asking for it. It just can't sustain you indefinitely.

The one upside of being in Georgia was that I was now closer to my mother's extended family in Dublin. For most of my life, I only had connections with my father's relatives in Georgia. After we were taken away from my mother, I'd never had the chance to meet her side of the family. On one of my mother's visits to our new home, we took a drive down to my old hometown, and

I met a slew of my cousins, aunts, and even my grandfather, who was at least seven feet tall. I was finally able to see where I'd gotten my height, and more important, the potential for my kids, particularly Shaquille, to be over seven feet tall. My grandfather died shortly after that visit, so I felt very blessed to have met him at least once. We all need that connection with family, even if just for a moment.

Back home, I was still struggling to keep everything up and running smoothly, which was not an easy task given how close in age my youngest children were. We managed somehow, but not without the occasional glitch. One such glitch turned my world and my marriage upside down.

I remember it quite vividly, as though it happened just yesterday. We had been in Georgia for about a year. I was in the kitchen, getting dinner ready while the children were playing in another room. Jamal was in his high chair near me. Phil came home early, as he sometimes did, and he took an immediate head count of the children as he always did. Ayesha, who was just two years old at the time, was not in the room, and the back sliding door was open. One moment she was there; the next moment she was gone.

I nearly lost my mind when Phil yelled out that Ayesha was missing. I'd been regularly checking in on them every few minutes like clockwork while I cooked dinner. I couldn't understand how she could have just walked away from us and right out the back door. I didn't even hear the sliding door open or close. But children will do just that sometimes, and it only takes a second for them to get away from you. Nevertheless, when Phil realized what had happened, he was livid and went about chastising, belittling, and hurling painful insults about my parenting skills toward me. He was spewing

the most hateful things he could think of as I stood there flabber-
gasted. Now, I was absolutely beside myself at the thought of my
baby being lost somewhere out there by herself. But he still felt he
needed to chew me out in the middle of my own worst nightmare.

Somehow Ayesha had wandered across the street and into the park.
Neighbors found her about forty-five minutes later and brought her
back home to us unharmed. I cried when I saw her and hugged her
little body so tight she had to pull away from me. She couldn't have
known that my tears weren't just for her. Phil had never lashed out
at me like that before. It tore me up inside to hear some of the mean
and nasty things he had to say. I was trying so hard to keep our
home together, with very little money, and had the added stressor
of having to cope with his absence for weeks at time while he was
on duty. A little piece of me just curled up and withered away that
day, and it would be years before I could reclaim it.

CHAPTER 18

New Marching Orders

Confess your trespasses to one another, and pray for one
another, that you may be healed.

—James 5:16 (NKJV)

A s with most disappointments, setbacks, and losses in life, you
have to pick yourself up and keep it moving, no matter how
heavily something is weighing on your heart. My marriage was
something that I cherished and wanted to work out at all costs.
To clear the air, I did try to discuss with Phil how hurt I'd been by
his tone and language during a particularly disturbing incident in
our family. A child going missing is hard on everyone, and yelling
at one another does nothing to help. I tried with all my might to
explain this to him, but as far as I could tell, my feelings didn't
seem to register with him at all. He felt he'd done nothing wrong,
and furthermore, since I was his wife, he felt it was his right to
speak to me in any way he chose.

Part of his antiquated thought process, I think, came from his father, a die-hard Jamaican who believed strongly that all men should be the heads of their households, with little input coming from the woman in the marriage. If that wasn't bad enough, the other part of my husband's stunted thinking was connected to his military training.

In the Army, it was all about rules and following those rules to the letter. Phil spent his days with people giving him orders, and other days he was the one giving the men in his command orders. I guess that type of work environment was hard for him to leave behind once the day was over, because when he came home, the children and I became soldiers in his own private platoon. The wrapping was coming off the very pretty package I'd received when we first married.

In fairness to Phil, he loved me the only way he knew how, and people do show and give love in vastly different ways. Similar to my grandparents and how they loved me from afar because of their backgrounds, Phil thought protecting me, giving me shelter, and putting food on the table was true love and good enough. And, when I married him at nineteen, I thought it was too.

But as the years passed by, I realized that love simply wasn't enough. I needed a partnership that included respect, communication, and compromise. Without those three things, love simply can't thrive or survive. So many young people today go into marriage thinking that love is all you need. I say, don't let the cute love songs fool you. I endured many things because I loved Phil, I loved my family, and I loved the life we were trying to create and sustain together. Would I be able to make it last? Who knew?

After spending four years in Georgia at Fort Stewart, we were given our orders to transfer to Germany. This meant we were finally getting the chance to leave the country and see the rest of the world, like I had always dreamed about doing.

Surprisingly, I had a rush of conflicting emotions once it began to sink in that we'd actually be leaving the States. Being separated from my family, particularly my mother, was going be painful. My mother had become my rock as I struggled to become what I thought was the perfect wife and mother. I relied on her wisdom and words of comfort to get me through each trying moment. Even if I just had a bad day with the kids, with one phone call she made it all seem so much better.

Not surprisingly, my relationship with my mother really flourished as I became an adult. She was so supportive and aware of the challenges I faced trying to juggle my growing responsibilities. Our long talks often involved her encouraging me to be more proactive in my life. I can still hear her voice saying, "Lou, stop being so pitiful." (My mother always called me Lou.) I had a tendency to feel sorry for myself when things seemed to be unraveling around me. She knew I had a strong foundation in Christ and tried to get me back on track with my connection with God. But after years of no one listening to me, this time around it was me who wasn't listening.

Though I'd be thousands of miles away from my mother, the one person who I felt really loved and understood me, I also longed to have the life my parents and grandparents were never able to have. To me, that meant a life with fewer limits and more options to explore different cultures, dialects, and people. Both Phil and I embraced the move wholeheartedly, anxiously looking forward to making the most of yet another new home. But, the feelings of my oldest child, Shaquille, told quite another story. He was nearly ten or eleven years old at the time. He'd made many friends at his school, and he didn't want to leave them behind. He also shared a tight bond with his grandmother and great-grandmother in New Jersey. The thought of leaving them all behind was completely unacceptable to him. My other children were still too young to fully understand what a big move we were about to undertake. But it was all too real for Shaquille.

CHAPTER 19

"Been Around the World"

A longing fulfilled is a tree of life.

—Proverbs 13:12

After spending a few weeks in New Jersey with family and friends, we all boarded the plane to head to Germany for what was supposed to be a three-year stay. Shaquille, who was sick with a head cold, cried the entire way, and that only made his bad cold even worse. He coughed and sobbed throughout the twenty-one-hour plane ride. I felt so bad for my baby that I cried too.

Germany was a brand-new world, and it took a fair amount of time for all of us to get accustomed to our new surroundings. Yes, we'd lived in New Jersey, where it gets pretty chilly, but nothing could have prepared us for Germany's brutal winters. To get a sense for just how cold it was, imagine something akin to the North Pole, and not the one with Santa Claus. But the winters were also breathtakingly beautiful. It was like looking at a postcard each time we looked out of our window. Good times!

Shaquille took his own sweet time warming up to his new home, but eventually all the kids were involved in enough extracurricular activities to fill their time so they were too occupied to miss home. Unfortunately, being worlds away in Germany did little to squash Shaquille's tendency to cause an uproar at school for his antics. One day he decided to teach the other kids in his homeroom how to break-dance. Understand, his teacher had never seen this urban dance before and thought Shaquille was having a seizure as he twirled again and again down on the floor. She called both Phil and me in a panic to ask that we come pick him up immediately and take him to the doctor. Now, both of us knew the boy was not having a seizure. He did break-dancing around the house all the time, with little notice from the rest of us. But he'd scared that little German teacher to death. We grounded Shaquille for a week after that incident, which thankfully did the trick for a while. Being stuck in the house was no fun for a teenager, and he hated not being able to go to the recreational center to play ball with his friends.

Phil did his best to spend his afternoons with the children, and he even began to work one-on-one with Shaquille on both his football and basketball skills. Shaquille hadn't yet decided which sport he preferred; back then he enjoyed both. Phil was an amazing father, and he truly loved his kids. He treated Shaquille like his own, which I'm so grateful for.

My first few weeks in Germany were spent setting up our new home and befriending the other mothers on the base. There was a pretty large African-American population stationed there, along with many people from all types of backgrounds. Race was a complete nonissue, which was somehow strange and wonderful all at the same time. It was as though we'd entered a land disconnected from the rest of the world. Having lived through the civil rights movement and watched as Dr. King and Robert Kennedy were assassinated, this was no small revelation for my eyes. Having the opportunity to see all types of people living among one another with little to no issues made me realize that racism is indeed a disease that can be cured. America just has to want to get better.

As the children became acclimated to their new home, Phil and I resumed our usual weekend house parties with the new families we'd met; we played cards on the weekends and drank our Saturday nights away with reckless abandon.

Drinking is amazingly fun while you're doing it. The next day, however, is quite another story. My typical Sunday mornings were filled with headaches, blurred vision, and a complete loss of memory. For the life of me, I could never completely recall all that had taken place the night before. My friends would later tell me how I'd get shamefully boisterous, loud, and feisty when I drank and got tipsy. They would detail how I'd even cussed out a few folks during my drunken nights and how I was apparently quick to tell Phil what I would and wouldn't do. Now, that was something I could never muster enough courage to do while sober. Of course, Phil drank, too, but he could handle his liquor a whole lot better than I could.

On the outside looking in, many may have considered my frequent drinking to be a problem, and to some extent it was. But back then I didn't think about it long enough to admit it. I felt like I was in control and handling my business, so it didn't occur to me it was a problem. My kids were fed, bathed, and settled in for the night before I'd begin sipping my Miller Lite or a glass of white wine to unwind.

Oh, how I remember nights when I would wander into Shaquille and Jamal's room while tipsy and belt out the song "Just a Closer Walk with Thee" in Shaquille's ear. I guess that was my version of an impromptu church service. My oldest son would just look at me for a minute and then roll over and put his pillow over his head to drown me out. Jamal usually just sat up in his bed with a bewildered look on his face. Ayesha and Lateefah would completely ignore me when I roamed into their room. My kids understood not to ask me any important questions while I was drinking, because I'd never remember my answer. I was very honest with them about my need to escape for just a few hours, sometimes even during the week. I tried to keep my drinking on school nights to a minimum so I would be available to my kids for help with homework and other things. But the weekends were all mine.

There is no doubt in my mind that the drinking became worse as the pressures and loneliness of being so far away from home, and especially from my mother, started to really close in on me. Because of the distance, phone calls were out of the question, but I wanted to hear my mother's soothing voice so badly. She wrote dutifully, fusing Scripture with encouraging words and support. I sometimes regret not writing her back more often during that time, or at least with a little more speed, but my life was way too chaotic for me to sit down and write a letter. Nonetheless, our bond was so strong that I could tell she felt my emptiness from all the way across the Atlantic Ocean.

While Germany eventually became a pleasant departure from the norm for us, sadly, it did not in any way improve our financial picture. Phil resisted the notion of me working while the children were still young, which made sense then. Day care alone would have eaten up any additional income I could make. My old-fashioned husband preferred I stay home, cook dinner, take care of the kids, and perform my other wifely duties with no outside distractions. That got old very quickly.

I had plenty of company with the other wives on the base who all found themselves stuck in the same rut of cooking, cleaning, and polishing military brass. We'd often meet at the playground and discuss the monotony of our days while we watched our children play. Those chats weren't particularly encouraging for me, because there seemed to be no light at the end of the tunnel. I had no desire to end up like many of those women, who'd spent their entire adult lives following their husbands from place to place, never able to create a life of their own. Again, I'm not judging the women who do make the military their life—I just knew it wasn't for me. I didn't know exactly how I was going to change my fate, but as my mother said to me in letter after letter, "God has the master plan."

Eventually I was able to persuade Phil that I needed to work to help out the family. Struggling to make ends meet was really taking a toll on me, though I made the most of it. Now, I did take pride in my ability to cut up an entire chicken thirteen ways for six people to eat—that was a true art. But dinners were getting harder to stretch out with four growing kids. In truth, I also wanted to get out on my own for a little while by leaving the house for a few hours during the day.

Since I knew I needed to work near home, I spent a few weeks on the base, filling out applications for every type of position I was qualified for. I'd always worked at some type of administrative job while working for the city in New Jersey, so secretary jobs, phone operator jobs, and anything else in that line of work I applied for. I got few callbacks, and finally I decided that my first job would be at a youth center on the base. It was perfect because it was where my kids also spent their time swimming and playing other sports. I could work and keep an eye on them at the same time.

The job was akin to a youth counselor, but because I was the last hired, I was the low man on the totem pole. That resulted in being assigned horrible hours—they even had me scheduled to work weekends, which would never do. That was family and Phil time. Needless to say, I didn't stay at that job for very long. It seemed I was going to have to search a little longer for my perfect fit in the working world, because this one wasn't exactly what I needed for my mental well-being or our pocketbooks. Thank goodness the kids had no idea we were struggling, and they were as happy as they could be with what we were able to provide for them. Therein lies the beauty of childhood. Children can sometimes be oblivious to the chaos that surrounds them.

CHAPTER 20

"The Best of My Love"

For our heart is glad in him, because we trust
in his holy name.

—Psalm 33:21 (ESV)

My need for outside stimulation wasn't the only issue I was facing while in Germany. I was also quietly struggling with a marriage that was, at least for me, continuing to be less than fulfilling, not that anyone could tell, of course. I went about my business as usual, being the dutiful wife and mother I'd always been, cooking, cleaning, and catering to every whim anyone in the family had.

My entire life revolved around my husband, my kids, and *their* happiness. This is something so many women do without even realizing it. We're programmed early on to only think of others. It was the same mind-set I'd always employed: go along to get along, and don't stir the pot. In truth and fairness, my husband, Phil, probably had no idea how unhappy I was, because I could never find the words to tell him unless I had a stiff drink in my hand.

The military had made my four children and me Phil's dependents. This meant he was in total control of everything we did and didn't do, a fact he took a little too literally for my taste. In his world I was no different than one of the children; we were all forced by the Army to pick up and move every few years and start all over again at the drop of a hat, all for *his* career and upward mobility. In his defense, I do think that this was the way Phil thought a healthy family should operate, with the man in charge and the head of all decisions. Unfortunately, he had somehow convinced himself that I felt exactly the same way. I didn't.

My repressed anger at our arrangement no doubt fueled my weekend drinking binges, which eventually became more cathartic than anything else. I could say what I wanted to say or be who I wanted to be, even if only for a few hours. It was my only escape, and everyone, including Phil, seemed to appreciate that I needed one badly. My kids, who rather enjoyed me in my drunken state, seemed to get it as well. At the very least they never complained.

There is one incident that still scares me when I think of what could have been. Phil was away on field duty (familiar story), and I needed to find a way to entertain the children over the weekend. Thankfully, there was a carnival on base, so I rounded the kids up, and we made our way there. With so much to do all over, the children ran from booth to booth to see what was inside. Since they were content, I went looking for my own contentment—which was located in a booth where the German beer was being served. Now, German beer is not like American beer in the least bit. It has much more of a kick, but in a more subtle way. You can drink and drink and never feel a thing until you stop. That's what happened that day, and when I felt I was good and plastered, I summoned the kids and drove home. What was I thinking? I had quite a buzz, but fortunately Jesus was at the wheel and got us all home safely.

Still, I wouldn't escape the day unscathed. Before I could get the kids into the house, my neighbor from across the street called out my name. I had no idea what she could have wanted, because we weren't friends, so to speak. And we certainly wouldn't be after that day. She proceeded to tell me that she'd seen me drink like a sailor that day and that I should be ashamed of myself, carrying on like that around kids. She then warned that if I ever did that again and drove with those kids in the car afterward, she'd report me. I sobered up real quick after hearing those words. I didn't exactly appreciate her tone, but she had a valid point. It wasn't enough to keep me sober permanently, but I never will forgot the chill that moved down my spine as I thought about the danger I'd potentially put my children in.

My four little ones were my pride and joy, so how could I put their lives in jeopardy? They were my godsends then as they are now. I'm not sure how I would have survived those years without them. My children were and still are the best part of me, and they provided distraction from everything I didn't like about my life and myself. Any parent knows what an amazing feeling it is to watch your offspring grow into their own personalities. What's equally fascinating is to realize that even with the same parents, kids can be so completely opposite from one another.

Take, for instance, my oldest daughter, Lateefah. She was always inquisitive as a child, but as an adult, she's a bit more hesitant in her own life than I would have guessed she'd be. She's my child who I have to really lift up high so she'll recognize her true gifts and talents. But that's what we mothers do for our children, isn't it? We are their loudest cheerleader, their best friend, and anything else they need.

Now, on the opposite end of the pole is my middle daughter, Ayesha. She was born prematurely and was always quiet and reserved as a child. But as an adult, she's been consistently fearless and determined. We've always called her our miracle child, and her strength still amazes me to this day. My youngest, Jamal, is the true baby of the family. As a child, he wouldn't leave my side, even when it was time to go to school. As an adult, he's still fighting the stigma of being the baby by doing things his way and stubbornly rejecting all advice. Be it right or wrong, he's going to do what he wants to do, and all I can do is just sit back and pray for the best.

Then there's my oldest child, Shaquille. He was the happiest baby and laughed all the time. He rarely cried and was never really sick—except for a cold now and then and the measles. My grandmother always referred to him as an "old soul," and rightly so. As a child, he was very willful and seemed to develop the traits of an adult as soon as he learned how to walk. It was as if he knew his height would cause people to think he was older, so he figured he might as well act it too. When he put his mind to accomplishing something, there was nothing anyone could do to stop him; he'd work until he got it done.

When I think of his long career in the NBA, I often reflect back to his childhood and when he first decided he wanted to become a professional basketball player. It seemed so far-fetched to me then, but Shaquille was always convinced it would happen. Part of my disbelief in him achieving his dream was connected to the fact that I was so preoccupied with the life I wasn't living. I couldn't see anything because I was so miserable. I didn't know what constituted a good marriage or true happiness, but I was pretty sure I didn't have either at that moment. I was doing exactly what my mother had asked me *not* to do: wallow in my own self-pity. I'd done that enough before to know that it was not only a complete waste of time, but that it can also blind you to the little things that are happening around you. I had to find a better way to handle my stress and disappointments before they took me under.

Finding a job would be one way to go. I continued to look for work during this time, and eventually I found a good job that I enjoyed a great deal, in the motor pool department of the Army. There I did mostly administrative work, like filling out request orders for car repairs, and services and answering the phones from nine to five. This worked perfectly for the kids, who were in school most of the day and then headed to the base recreational center until I reached home. Shaquille was a teenager by then, so he could handle things if I happened to be late. I tried to make sure that didn't happen very often. It can indeed be easy, when there is one child much older than the others, to put them in charge and forget that they're children as well. I didn't want him to have that responsibility as a teenager. I wanted him to enjoy his childhood because he'd be an adult soon enough. My new job wasn't the beginning of a long career, but it made me feel like I was finally contributing more than just clean clothes to the family's well-being.

I also managed to make some pretty good friends there, like Frau Buettner. I have no idea what her first name was, because we only referred to each other using our last names. Frau Buettner was a mature woman who frequently brought in delicious home-made German dishes and gave me the recipes to prepare them at home. When I did take a chance to try one, the kids usually loved them. Anything to avoid more chicken à la king.

CHAPTER 21

The Family
That Plays Together . . .

Where your treasure is, there your heart will be also.

—Matthew 6:21

While Phil initially frowned on my working outside the home, there were no complaints when the extra money began trickling in. Now at least our phone could stay connected (it was frequently turned off because of long-distance calls back home), and the children, who all grew like weeds in the middle of every summer, could have the extra clothes and shoes they needed for school.

It was also during this time that Shaquille began to gain some local attention for his sports acumen. He'd developed a nice little following as he played basketball for the American high school team on the base and as he traveled around Germany, playing in different tournaments. Those times were particularly worrisome for me because I had no idea where he was going in a country that was still foreign to us. What if something were to go wrong on one of his trips? What if he got sick? How could we get to him, and how would we even know where to go? Despite regularly being in the middle of one of my drunken weekend stupors, I'd stay up late into the night during his trips, waiting until I saw the bus drive up and Shaquille's head round the corner near our home. Only then could I go to sleep in peace.

When he did play on base, the entire family would go to every game to cheer him on. It was very refreshing and cute to watch him find his way on the court. His height, of course, was a plus, but basketball is much more than how tall you are. Learning plays, coordination, and other physical skills is needed to really excel in high school and beyond. The games in Germany were usually against other kids on the base. His games against other schools took place off the base, and that made it difficult for all of us to attend. After his trips, Shaquille would give the family play-by-play descriptions of the opposing team and how the game progressed quarter by quarter. He also loved to describe the area and how beautiful each particular city or town was he played in. We'd sit and listen for hours.

Though my marriage wasn't exactly headed in the direction I hoped, Phil and I remained on the same page when it came to parenting. I cannot give Phil enough credit for being the loving, supportive, and involved father he was to all our children. I've been around long enough to know that not all men take their parental responsibilities seriously.

Being on the same page also meant we both felt strongly about teaching our children that school was the only avenue to a better life. While Phil attended college for a few years, I hadn't had the chance to go right after high school, but we certainly expected our children to do so.

Now, given our financial situation, it was unclear how we'd pay for that education, but as parents, we were committed to finding a way. I wanted our children to have the options and choices I didn't have just as I had options my mother and father didn't have. My way of thinking is that each generation has a responsibility to go further than the one before, and our way of getting them there is to give our children guidelines to follow.

All four of our kids loved sports and participated in all types on the weekends and after school. It was so wonderful watching them make friends and enjoy healthy competition with other kids. But we still enforced the steadfast rule of "no pass, no play" in our house. Even as Shaquille became more and more dominant as a player in high school circles, we insisted he get good grades, for his sake and for the possibility of a scholarship. We preached that his physical talent was no more important than the strength of his mind, and he needed both to really capitalize on opportunities. Young athletes today often don't get this lesson, and I believe they eventually go on to regret it. I'm also convinced that my son continues to be a success in the NBA and in the business world because he took his studies as seriously as he took basketball.

We really did share many happy family times together in Germany. When both of our daughters were playing basketball or cheering on the sidelines as they got older, I'd often step in as the team's mother or cheerleading coach. Phil would teach and coach football and basketball when both Shaquille and his brother, Jamal, played. This kept us together constantly and connected us through mutual interests. No matter what activity the children were interested in, either Phil or I would accompany them and try to be as supportive as we could, whenever we could.

Sticking together as a family would become even more imperative as Shaquille's face became well-known around the base. It got to the point where all we had to do was go grocery shopping and people would just reach out to him and literally pull him away from the rest of the family to talk basketball. It was a little scary to have complete strangers come up out of nowhere and basically accost your child. To combat this, we began to walk together with Shaquille in the middle of all of us, to avoid people separating us as a unit. We didn't know what some of those people really wanted with Shaquille, and whatever it was, we weren't interested.

With so much attention coming Shaquille's way, Phil and I went to great lengths to make sure our other children got the focus and the attention they deserved. This is something we always did throughout their lives, particularly because they were so close in age. It was a given that now as more and more attention was being concentrated on Shaquille, we needed to give them even more of our time. We had no idea what the future would hold for our oldest son; we just knew that all our children had to get the encouragement they needed from us if they were to succeed. The four of them always had such a wonderful relationship with each other, and we wanted that to continue with no friction, jealousy, or competition. Also, perhaps more than the average person, I knew how fragile a child's self-esteem could be, so I wanted to be absolutely sure all of them felt loved and appreciated for who they were and not who we thought they should be.

I have so many fond memories of Shaquille spending his

Sunday mornings (before Phil and I got up with our hangovers) entertaining his brothers and sisters with cereal, pillow fights, and silly dance performances. As a mother, you want your children to bond in that way, and can only pray that they remain close as they continue to get older.

Phil and I explained to them that each child had his or her own pathway and that all four of them would have bright futures, but in their own special way. Again, I still hadn't given the slightest thought to the future success or fame Shaquille might actually achieve; I just knew that I wanted all my children to love themselves no matter what. Nothing was more important to me than that. Even now, I think Shaquille's success has been the hardest on his brother, Jamal, my youngest child and only other son. Because of this, both Phil and I spent a great deal of time over the years with him, encouraging him not to pattern his life after his older brother. What has made it particularly difficult for Jamal is that he is 6'8" and built just like Shaquille, body wise. With his height, my youngest son is constantly asked why he isn't on a team, playing ball, like his brother. People can be so cruel, never considering the fact that just maybe he didn't want to play basketball. I've felt his pain over years as he's dealt with the questions and stares. But I continued to reassure him that he would be his own man someday and find his place in the world.

So many expectations are put on our children by others, and that certainly has been the case with all my children in the wake of Shaquille's success. I didn't know what they'd face as they were growing up, but I'm so glad Phil and I made it a point to prepare them. Sometimes at night I'd read each of my children one of my favorite writings by author Roy Lessin. I don't even remember where I read this poem, but when I saw it the first time, it touched me to my soul. It's the story of God telling one of his followers how each life is different. Here's an excerpt:

"The Pathway"

The pathway you see is the path that I have chosen and prepared for you. Follow it with confidence, trust and courage. It will perfectly lead you into plans I have for your life. If you ever wonder where the pathway is taking you, simply look down and you will notice my footsteps in front of you. As you walk you will notice other pathways close to yours. Some will draw your interest and curiosity. You may be attached because of the flowers that border them, trees that shade them, or the direction in which they are heading. What you don't see is the depth of the valleys, and the steepness of the mountains through which they wind. Those whom I have called to travel these pathways will have my grace for their journey. I do not want you to waste your time imagining what it might be like traveling down someone else's path. If you choose another's path, you will not have my grace upon you, and the valleys and hills will burden you and create weariness within you. The time and energy I give you will always be enough for each day's travel, and you will find many resting places along the way. Give yourself completely to the path I have prepared for you. As you do, continue to look upon MY face, for my smile will be upon you. I know where the path will take you, for I already traveled it. Believe me when I say that you can never imagine the incredible things that await you.

CHAPTER 22

"A Change Is Gonna Come"

You need to persevere so that when you have done the
will of God, you will receive what he has promised.

—Hebrews 10:36

After spending an additional year in Germany with the hope of increasing Phil's opportunities for a higher rank, we finally got the news that we'd be heading back to the United States in the summer of 1987. We would be stationed in Texas. There aren't enough words in the English language to describe how overjoyed I was that I'd finally be able to reconnect with my mother and the rest of my family after four long years of separation. Ironically, we'd all grown to love Germany, the people, and even the weather to some extent; but it wasn't home, and it never would be. The children were growing up so fast, and Shaquille was already in high school. I wanted all my kids to get back to the world they'd actually live in as adults, and that was in America.

But, as with anything in life, the transition back home was not without its rough patches. No, there weren't any alligator tears this time on the plane, but we were in for a culture shock of major proportions once we landed back on U.S. soil. While it wasn't uncommon for people in Germany to stare in amazement at Shaquille because of his height (he was 6'8" by the time he was fourteen years old) or reach out to touch my daughter's hair after I'd put cornrows in, we were basically treated with kindness and respect the entire time we were overseas. I didn't have to worry about racial profiling when my boys left the house, or racial slurs being thrown at my girls when they were attending school. Back home, it would be an entirely different story. We were going to have to adjust all over again to a world where the way you looked meant everything, and the color of your skin could (if you allowed it) determine where you ended up in life. My children were too young to understand that ugly truth before we left the country, and they'd been spoiled by the open-mindedness of foreigners. Somehow I would have to explain to them why people, divided by only a large body of water, could think and treat each other so differently.

After a few weeks of spending time getting reacquainted with friends and family back in New Jersey (I think I hugged my mother for an hour straight), we made the trek to Fort Sam Houston in San Antonio, Texas. Because Phil was nearing his fifteenth year in the Army and winding down his career, this would be the last major move we'd make at the military's behest. Thankfully, it was with relative ease that I was able to find another civil service job that once again helped the family make ends meet. We still struggled to pay the bills every month, as we did at every stop, but somehow we got by.

During the winter months, near the holidays, we'd often borrow money from the local bank so we could afford to buy the kids their Christmas gifts and clothes. I don't recall exactly what eight hundred dollars actually bought back then, but I do remember one Christmas when Shaquille was about ten years old; he wanted (and received) that funny-looking Stretch Armstrong doll. You know, the one where you could pull the doll's arms and legs all the way out because he was made of some kind of waxy material? Well, Shaquille played with that doll for one day only (Christmas), until he pulled the poor thing and it tore completely open. My child had no idea of his own strength.

Texas proved to be an easy mix with the kids' personalities, and I had no problems getting back into my old familiar routine of surviving, drinking, and then surviving again. I'd pretty much accepted the day-to-day lifestyle associated with being an Army spouse, and I don't recall it being much like that Lifetime show *Army Wives*.

Phil and I were continuing to grow apart, even though I don't think he really noticed. He couldn't see how, quietly, I was hurting inside. That's just how quiet it was. Despite having the family I'd always wanted, I still felt incomplete. I hated the fact that even with the wonderful titles of mother and wife, it still wasn't enough. That kind of emptiness comes when you don't have love for yourself, and while I was getting older, I wasn't getting any better in that department.

In reality, my unhappiness wasn't Phil's fault or anyone else's. As women, we often look to our men to be the knights in shining armor who will make everything right. We expect them to be the ones to validate us and make us feel worthy. Trust me when I say, the men in our lives can't do that. More often than not, they are fighting the same insecurities and demons we are. It would take me years to realize that I was the only one responsible for my happiness and that blaming others only shifted the focus away from where it needed to be—on me. I had to figure out for myself the root of my pain so that I could make it stop. But I still had a ways to go before I'd find the answer.

Nevertheless, as a couple, we carried on and quickly connected with a new round of friends who just loved coming over to our house for drinks, cards, and any other weekend escapes we could muster up. I loved the fact that while all of us had financial problems (enlisted soldiers make very little), that never stopped us a bit from having all the liquor we wanted when we were in the mood to drink. If Phil and I didn't have a good enough supply, the couple next door would donate it, or the family down the street would bring the extra six-pack of beer to make the night complete.

As we resumed the life we'd always lived from the old base to the new one, things were changing rapidly for Shaquille. Though he'd made a name for himself in Germany with his impressive basketball skills, moving to Texas was akin to starting all over again. He'd have to prove himself at a school and in a country where basketball was not just a sport but a religion, with a lot better talent. Still, my son was undeterred, as he was with most things in life. Of course, there were times when his confidence was rattled, like when the newspapers questioned early on whether this very tall man-child could walk and chew gum at the same time or even actually help the base high school team (Cole High School) get to the state championship.

Those local sports stories would be our first foray into the world of media, and it was also the beginning of a very long and complicated relationship we as a family would have with the press, which still continues today. It's hard not to fight back tears when I think about some of the painful and untrue things the press has said about us over the years. I don't even want to repeat some of the untrue stories that have been printed. Not all the press are unfair, of course; most reporters and writers have been very fair. But there have always been a few that do whatever it takes to sell papers. We've all learned how to grin and bear it, but it's been one of the most difficult adjustments we've had to make. I'm really not going to miss that part of our lives when Shaquille retires.

In Germany, it had been pretty much a big love fest between Shaquille and the Army newspaper, *Stars and Stripes*. With his talent and skill, he could do no wrong in their eyes. Back in the United States, he was in the real world of sports, where scholarships were won and potential NBA careers were born, so Shaquille would get no mercy. His only saving grace was to blow their socks off during his basketball games (which he did), and he helped his team win a state championship. That was an incredible experience for the entire family as we followed him from city to city and watched his team bring the championship trophy home. I think the kids had the best time traveling on the road like a superstar rock group.

For some reason, despite all of Shaquille's success, I was still struggling with processing the fact that my son was on his way to becoming a star NBA player. Yes, I knew it was his dream, and he'd worked very hard to make it happen. But all I ever wanted for all of my children was the opportunity for them to go to school, continue on to get their degrees, and then get good jobs. I never thought about them being rich or famous; I just wanted them to be happy and well-adjusted. I didn't have any objection to fame and fortune, mind you, it just wasn't very high on my list of priorities as I was raising them. I could see clearly that Shaquille had an opportunity for a basketball scholarship because of his skills, and God knows I was thankful for that.

But reality hit me dead in the face when I saw him play on national television for the first time. I remember it so well. We'd invited as many friends as we could over to our house to watch Shaquille play in the McDonald's All-American Game. That game is the biggest high school competition around, and only the best players in the country compete. We were serving barbecue and beer in the backyard while the game played on our outside television, which was sitting under a large tent that Phil borrowed from the Army warehouse.

My plan that day was to get very plastered as the afternoon and game played on, and I was a woman of my word. To keep things entertaining, every single time my son hit a shot or showed up on the screen, I took the opportunity to act a true fool by cheering nonstop and pointing constantly while saying, "Look at my boy," pretending the people at the party didn't know that was my son. Now, I admit I was very drunk and feeling mighty fine that day, but part of my performance was real. I was beginning to come to grips with a reality that was approaching me like a speeding bullet. God knows I was far from ready for what was just around the corner.

CHAPTER 23

Good Intentions

Faith is being sure of what we hope for
and certain of what we do not see.

—Hebrews 11:1

Somehow, I would have to find a way to clean up my act quickly, as the prospects for Shaquille's future would soon come knocking on our door. Colleges from around the country were interested in him, and in the news and on the sports radio shows, there was nonstop action and chatter about which college he'd end up attending. All of the attention we began receiving was absolutely surreal for us as a family.

Now, the coaches and colleges can only recruit at certain times of the year, so we did get breaks here and there. As parents, Phil and I were involved in meeting the different coaches at the end of Shaquille's senior year, something Phil took a shine to immediately. He relished asking all the questions and grilling prospective coaches and school officials on everything that was in store for Shaquille if he indeed chose their school. Some of the coaches that came by to wine and dine us were hilarious at best. One or two came with their younger "secretaries" for overnight visits, while others intentionally talked down to us, assuming that a black family from Jersey would never understand the intricate details of college sports. Phil really lit into those guys, letting them know in no uncertain terms that underestimating our intelligence wasn't going to endear them to our son. For the most part, I would let Phil handle all the talking—that is, until he got too upset and lashed out at the men a little too harshly. Phil could be a verbal serial killer if you gave him the chance, and God knows I knew how it felt to be on the receiving end. When things got a little too tense, I'd speak up in an effort to smooth things over and get back to discussing the best interests of our son. That took all the confidence I could summon. Those men and meetings petrified me to no end! I was so afraid that we *didn't* really understand the intricate details of college sports, and somehow Shaquille would be shortchanged because of it.

As we slowly adapted to the newfound attention, I began to attract what I liked to call "new friends." These "new friends" were people that had shown no interest in us before but now suddenly found it necessary to be at all of Shaquille's games. They would even find their way over to our house whenever they saw an opportunity. Even our younger children began to collect these hangers-on. These "friends" followed their every move and couldn't get enough of hearing about Shaquille and his games. Nothing is more difficult than explaining to your children the difference between true friends and insincere friends. I personally had never had the experience of having so many people with hidden agendas come my way. I was having my own hard time navigating between what was real and what wasn't. Sadly, this would be only the tip of the iceberg, since Shaquille would go from high school champion to college standout and NBA superstar within the space of about three years. The "faux friend movement" didn't just end with our immediate family. My entire extended family all the way back in New Jersey were also experiencing what it was like to have long lost friends and family coming out of the woodwork in droves because of Shaquille's success on the basketball court.

During this fast-moving time, I had no idea that God was really trying to speak to me. I didn't know how to listen to Him back then. I was too drunk on the weekends and too confused during the week to even consider the fact that God never abandons us. The liquor affected my hearing and my vision, but God kept on talking. It is clear to me now that even in 1988, God wanted me to know that once we decide to make Him the Lord of our lives, He orders everything that happens to us, and for us.

In Jeremiah 29:11, God is speaking to us and saying, "For surely I know the plans I have for you . . . to . . . give you a future with hope" (NRSV). God's plan has all the benefits we'll ever need: a future with hope, free from the hold of sin and death. And with this new freedom we've been adopted into God's family, with full rights and a share in Jesus' inheritance. What a revelation!

As things began to spiral out of control, with so much changing in our family, I was so grateful for my mother's continued presence. Not only did she visit us as often as she could, but she also held my hand as I tried to navigate the chaos around me. I had one child on the verge of something great, and three others still needing me to guide them toward their futures. There were some days when I didn't know if I was coming or going. Even though my mother couldn't attend all of Shaquille's games, I made sure to send her the newspaper clippings, magazine articles, and anything else that focused on his burgeoning career.

Lord knows I needed that connection with my mother for other reasons as well. There were many days when I felt just like Joseph in the Bible, so disconnected from my other family members, especially Roy and Vivian. The communication had gotten so poor between us that our relationships with one another were virtually nonexistent. The rift between us had actually begun years before while I was still thousands of miles away, living in Germany. During those four years, only my mother kept in regular contact. I tried to reach out to my siblings, but our phone was regularly disconnected because of the cost, and sitting down and writing a detailed letter was a hard task to complete with four young kids, although I did manage a few times.

On the occasions that I did try to reach out to them, I never heard back. I would write to ask them if they could send shoe and clothing catalogs to me for the kids. Shaquille was growing out of everything we'd bought him, and it had gotten to the point where I simply couldn't find clothes or shoes that fit him in Germany. America always had a much better selection for his size. I was at my wits' end and truly at a loss for what to do. When I got no word from them, I of course thought the worst. I interpreted their silence as a total rejection and dismissal of me. I never once considered that they had families of their own and were struggling just as much as we were. The only conclusion I could come to was that they didn't care about my children or me at all. We were so far from home, and any form of contact would have meant the world to us. They had each other, since they lived in the same city; couldn't they see that? But in reality, they had no way of understanding what we were dealing with in Germany. I was the first in the family to the leave the country or even just the North, so they couldn't understand the isolation and detachment that comes with being thousands and thousands of miles away. It feels like having a part of your body removed, but you have to keep going. I just thank the Lord that no family emergency occurred while I was so far away. We didn't have the resources to get back home in such a short time, and no one to help us.

My saving grace remained the visits from my mother, who took her vacation time to come to visit us everywhere, except when we were out of the country, and on one occasion she even brought my grandmother and cousins too. It was during this time that I found out the same thing Joseph eventually learned: what the enemy meant for evil in my life, God had turned around right before my eyes, even though I could barely see. Everything I had gone through and was going through in my life had been done for my own good! It was most certainly God saying, "I know the plans I have for you." God wanted me to know that although I had a bevy of problems and personal issues going on within, this was still a sure indication that a promise He gave me was about to be fulfilled. My future was filled with hope.

Sometimes we question whether God has made up His mind about blessing us. I know I did, and that was because I was still in that mental welfare state of mind. If only I'd known as a younger woman what I know now, I wouldn't have worried at all, because worry is a rejection of faith, and it's an insult to God. I needed to trust God and remain doubt free. Even when there were people all around me with hidden agendas (like there still are now), God sees all. Today I am always reminded not to worry about anything every time my cell phone rings. My ring tone is Isaiah 54:7, "No weapon . . . formed against thee shall prosper" (KJV). Just hearing those words daily lifts my spirit up another notch.

CHAPTER 24

Let the Games Begin

Hebrews 11:1 reminds us that "faith is the substance of things hoped for, the evidence of things not seen" (KJV), and, needless to say, I had some *crazy faith* stored deep down inside of me. There was enough faith in me to know that my baby boy was about to realize his lifelong dream; however, there were some days I was ignorant enough to be walking around like I was living in a nightmare. Everything was so overwhelming, and I could not keep up!

Thank goodness Phil and I always raised our children to make their own decisions on the issues that mattered the most to them. That's exactly what Shaquille did when it came time to choose the college he'd attend. As his parents, we'd heard it all, seen it all, and been promised it all by anybody and everybody on the college level; but ultimately it would be Shaquille leaving home, going to classes, and running up and down the court. We didn't get to accompany him on his visits to college campuses around the country during the established recruiting periods, but he'd return with the most vivid details of how beautiful the cities were and the incredible incentives they offered to convince him to attend the school. Some of the wining and dining was quite generous and could have easily caused Shaquille to fall for something that wasn't as it seemed or that would not have been good for him in the long run. But Phil and I constantly preached to our son that he should avoid signing anything while away on these trips. We couldn't always travel with him, and we most certainly did not want him to get in any kind of trouble with NCAA rules and regulations. One wrong move and Shaquille's professional future could have been jeopardized. The sporting world's news regularly reported incidents regarding well-known players whose colleges were penalized because of their inappropriate acceptance of gifts or money.

While the ultimate decision of where Shaquille would attend college was his alone, we did want to help. We used our weekly family meetings to examine the many books, cards, and letters that Shaquille received in the mail, and then we discussed the various possibilities each option offered. This gave our other children a chance to be involved in all of the excitement their older brother was experiencing. It also introduced them to the college decision process years before they'd need to figure out where they would attend.

I was relieved to let my son choose his own school, because I'd been impressed with so many of them after doing my own research that I never would have been able to narrow it down to just one institution. When he ultimately chose Louisiana State University (LSU) as his final destination, I don't think anyone in the entire family was taken by surprise. We were just thankful that he had been able to make up his mind given how overwhelming the entire recruiting process had been and all the different options available to him.

LSU was really the obvious choice from the beginning. Years before, while we were still stationed in Germany, the coach of LSU's men's basketball team, Dale Brown, visited the Army base in Wildflecken, West Germany, where we lived. He was there to give motivational speeches to the soldiers. On one particular Saturday, while taking a break in the program, Shaquille approached Coach Brown and asked, "Sir, can you give me some exercises that will help me build up my lower extremities?" Looking up at Shaquille and seeing how tall he was, the coach immediately asked, "What's your rank, soldier?" After a quick chuckle, Shaquille told him he was only fourteen years old. Coach Brown didn't even try to conceal his disappointment; he just knew he had a prospective player for his team, standing tall right there in front of him. They both had a good laugh about the mix-up, and Shaquille introduced the coach to Phil, who was nearby. A long-lasting relationship was formed that day, and though we didn't speak to the coach regularly, he would always send Christmas cards to my mother's house each year. Her address was our permanent stateside address.

The memory of the kindness he showed that day stayed with Shaquille and the rest of us long after, so it was a no-brainer that Shaquille would lean toward someone we all knew and trusted if and when the opportunity presented itself. Isn't it amazing how seeds of the future can be planted with just one chance meeting? Coach Brown's introduction to our lives was God's divine intervention in its truest form.

For those of who you haven't experienced this, there's nothing more numbing than your first child leaving home for college. It's an emptiness that's familiar to so many parents, yet it's still so hard to put into words. Their departure is all at once exhilarating and frightening as they begin a new chapter in their lives. I was obviously overjoyed that my son was beginning a new life with the chance for a bright future, but the selfish mother in me wanted to go back in time a few years. I wanted to return to the days when he was a young boy and I had to fight with bus drivers who didn't believe my son was still underage, or when we used to have to go from store to store to find shoes to fit his ever-growing feet every few months. What mother doesn't wish that time could hold still for just a little while longer? There was a moment when I would have done just about anything to avoid him leaving the nest. This was the child who had made me a mother for the first time. He was also the child that I was chastised for endlessly before his birth because I'd sinned and I wasn't married to his father.

Now, eighteen years later, he was on his way to what seemed to be the most amazing future of anyone in our family. He was making history, and I was so very proud of him. I always knew my baby was a blessing of unknown proportions, and now I was witnessing it firsthand. Of course, that didn't stop me from crying my eyes out the day we packed up his belongings.

On that fateful Friday afternoon, Phil and I drove him to Louisiana, where we spent the weekend with our son, setting him up in an off-campus apartment with his roommates. During the long, seven-hour car ride, I tried my best not to let my son or Phil see me wiping tears from my eyes. I pretended to have something in them or to yawn. They must have thought I was mighty sleepy. We spent the weekend with him to make sure he had all he needed. On Saturday, I headed to my favorite store, Kmart, to purchase glasses, sheets, and pillows for his new place.

Yes, Shaquille did leave, as most of our children do at some point, and somehow as mothers we manage to survive. I had three other children to focus on, and no matter what my emotional state, they still needed all the attention I could give them as they entered into their teen years.

CHAPTER 25

The Emptier Nest

All your sons will be taught by the LORD, and great will
be your children's peace.

—Isaiah 54:13

Life at home was as crazy and normal as it could be, though we
were now down one child. Phil and I continued to be dutiful parents, shuttling the kids back and forth to school, basketball
practice, cheerleading practice, and any other youth activity they
wanted to become involved in. Those activities kept me sane and
helped me keep my mind off the child who wasn't there.

My relationship with my husband also carried on as it always
had. Phil continued to be in control of every decision made in our
home, and I continued to step back and allow it. His career in the
Army was slowly coming to a close. Since his time in the military
was nearing an end, we were fortunate that, as a result, he wasn't
deployed to Iraq during Desert Storm in the early '90s. But as he

looked forward to retirement with some reservation, I was looking forward to a change coming into my life as well.

Now, I couldn't tell anyone the actual thoughts I was having
at that time because I was still in the process of questioning so
many things that no one could answer but me—like when would
I finally grow up and stand up for myself on the inside and the
outside? I was also trying to determine what I could do to change
my circumstances in ways that were best for everyone. Those were
tough questions for me to ask myself, and even tougher questions
for me to answer.

When I got tired of asking questions I didn't have the answers
to, I just reached for my old, faithful friend—the bottle. A drink
asks no questions and accepts you as you are. That's the power it
has over you—it meets you where you are and does its best to keep
you there. A drink never disappoints.

I continued to hold all of my angry emotions inside of me. Phil
and I simply didn't talk about what was bothering either of us. In
truth, I don't think I could have explained what I was feeling to
him anyway, because I didn't completely understand it all myself.
So much of what I was experiencing was deeply rooted in my low
self-esteem, which came as a direct result of my painful childhood
that I had yet to come to terms with. It was much easier to blame
my job, my family, and even Phil for how I was feeling, since he
was the closest person to me and because at times he made me feel
like a soldier in his platoon.

My mind wanders back to those times so much now because
of the many young military couples I see on the news every day.
Hot-topic news shows regularly focus on the stress of military life
and its impact on the lives of the families, particularly in the wake

of the Iraq War. That was the life we led for many years. No, Phil didn't fight in a war, but he was often away from us for long periods of time on field duty. When he was gone, it was a hardship on everyone. It really took its toll on Phil and his entire personality, which of course trickled down to the home front.

His absence instantly made me the temporary single parent of four, and that was no easy task, particularly when he was gone for extended periods of time. I would think to myself, *Is this what I signed up for? Being both the mother and father?* Because of my mental welfare, I'd depended on Phil for everything, and suddenly I would be in complete charge and on my own, and then like clockwork—I wasn't anymore. This left me in a constant state of confusion as I struggled to move back and forth between those two extremes.

Still, our time in the Army was a godsend for us, as it is for many families. Those years were filled with many wonderful moments, and the military did what it could to support the entire family unit during times of war and peace. In fact, the military is so supportive of spouses that I even received a certificate of appreciation when Phil retired. But different personalities handle separation, pressure, and stress in vastly different ways. Some of our friends in the service thrived on the challenges the military posed, while others crumbled under the pressure.

I'm not sure where Phil and I stood on that list, and back then I was too mired in my own self-pity to figure it out. I was still regularly throwing back drinks, and that only clouded my mind and judgment that much more. Even more disturbing than my drinking was the fact that money was still a major issue in the household. We faced an added pressure of knowing that now our oldest child was hundreds of miles away, struggling to get by as well. We had no money to send to Shaquille, like many parents do when their kids go off to school, and that hurt me so much as a mother. Though my connection to God was still a little strained, I spoke to Shaquille regularly about relying on God to get him through those tough times on campus when he didn't have what he needed. With little money and having to prove his basketball skills again on the tough college level, my son was dealing with a lot, and I felt so helpless being so far away from him. Still, I had to be encouraging, because there was nothing more important to me than Shaquille getting his degree.

I do regret not having the knowledge of Scripture then that I have now. There've been so many times that I read the Bible and see Scriptures that would have been perfect to read to my son during those trying times. Proverbs 4:10–13 would have indeed been perfect: "Listen, my son, accept what I say, and the years of your life will be many. I guide you in the way of wisdom and lead you along straight paths. When you walk, your steps will not be hampered; when you run, you will not stumble. Hold on to instruction, do not let it go; guard it well, for it is your life."

One thing is for sure: being broke will certainly force you to be a bit more creative in your thinking. Once a month we'd skip paying a major bill, like the rent; grab the kids; and hit the road. We'd make our way to Baton Rouge, Louisiana, where Shaquille was in school. We'd do some sightseeing in the area; catch a football game; eat some shrimp, crawfish and gator; and go watch Shaquille play ball during the basketball season. Those were great times, even though to get there it usually meant driving all night for seven hours, and then all five of us were jam-packed into one very small and very cheap hotel room. Later on we'd stay at the home of some of Shaquille's friends, which eased our financial situation enough to visit a bit more frequently. Eventually, Shaquille got a little summer job off campus and bought a piece of car that he'd drive home on some weekends and holidays. He christened his new Ford Explorer the "clunk-a-funk" because he played the music so loud you could hear him coming around the corner.

Shaquille broke tons of records at LSU while he played there, and that only fueled national interest in his future. As a family, those were some of the best times we shared, and I treasure them to this day.

We continued to take those monthly trips to Louisiana until the day I got the phone call that the entire family had been expecting for years. It was a Wednesday morning when the phone rang at my desk. Shaquille was on the other end when I picked up, and he said in his deepest, most serious voice, "Mommy, it's time. I want to make myself eligible for the upcoming NBA draft." After taking a second to absorb the announcement that he'd be leaving college after his junior year, I congratulated him but immediately made him promise me that he would return to college and complete his degree as soon as he possibly could. Thankfully, I got no argument, because Shaquille, like all my children, knew exactly how important education was to me.

Though I wanted him to finish college and get his degree, I also understood the world of sports. I knew that timing was everything when it came to entering the NBA: If you jump in too soon, you risk being too immature and unskilled to flourish. If you wait too long, you risk injury—or worse. In 1992, Shaquille felt that the time was right and that he was ready to spread his wings in the professional world of basketball. All I could do was pray that he was right. I knew in my heart that he'd outgrown the college game. I also felt he was ready for life in the NBA. But was the NBA ready for him?

As overwhelmed and taken aback as we were with the hoopla we faced while in Germany and during Shaquille's high school and college years playing ball, that would be like child's play compared to what we would soon face. The odd thing for me was that it should have been a time when the entire family was on top of the world, but all I felt was fear (as if I needed one more negative emotion to deal with). Fear of what? you might ask. My son was on his way to fame and fortune untold, but all I could focus on was, what if it all fell through? What if he got hurt before he even played his first game, and all of his dreams were shattered in an instant? How would he survive that?

It's not like it hadn't happened before. Look back over the years, and take note of some of the players that were the talk of the town before entering the league. Many indeed lived up to the hype and gained worldwide fame, but many more burned out, and with little fanfare to notice. Trust me: there are countless other young, talented, and bright athletes with that same story. What if that happened to my son too? What can I say? I'm a mother's mother. I worry about any and everything, and so many unforeseen things happen in this world that can change a life overnight with little rhyme or reason. Being a mother through and through, that's all I could think about. But I put on my best brave front when I was around the kids and Phil. The last thing I wanted to do was put a damper on my son's happiness and future. I simply planned to handle my fear the way I handled most of the unpleasant things in my life; I'd ignore it.

✳

CHAPTER 26

Eyes Wide Open

I waited patiently for the LORD to help me,

and he turned to me and heard my cry.

—Psalm 40:1 (NLT)

After Shaquille made the decision to enter the NBA draft, we knew we'd have to wait patiently to learn where he'd actually land and if he'd go first in the overall draft. The odds were in his favor that he'd be taken first by a team, given his stellar college and high school records. He'd gotten tons of attention in the media for his play, and things looked good for him being on top. Of course, it all would come to down to what team needed a center the most, but it also would come down to the luck of the draw. Traditionally, the team with the worst record from the year before gets to pick first.

I still remember beaming with pride that June afternoon while sitting in the Rose Garden in Portland, Oregon. Many of my family members made the trip with us. My mother was overcome with joy as well. My sister and brother couldn't take off of work that day, but I felt their presence in the room. My oldest son was about to be taken first in the 1992 NBA draft, and I couldn't have been more pleased. Shaquille's ear-to-ear grin just about said it all; his big smile lit up the room the moment NBA league commissioner, David Stern, announced that the Orlando Magic would be his new home and team.

The great Harlem Renaissance poet and writer Langston Hughes spoke about a dream deferred, but my God, what a glorious feeling it was to have one realized! The city known as home to Mickey and Minnie would now also be the home for Shaquille and the rest of our family as well. For nearly twenty years, Phil, the kids, and I had moved from place to place, like any military family is required to do. The day Shaquille entered the NBA signaled the end of all that. Phil retired, and we decided to settle down in one place, which turned out to be Orlando. We were all thrilled to finally have one place to call home, and what a very fine home it proved to be. We were also looking forward to enjoying the year-round warm weather that Orlando had to offer.

During Shaquille's first year in the NBA, Phil took center stage doing interviews and sound bites, which he seemed to truly enjoy. I was much more comfortable being the point person behind the scenes. Harking back to my younger days, I never much liked the spotlight, and shied away from it whenever I could. Instead, I went about the business of researching Orlando and finding a house for Shaquille. I also found another house for the rest of the family nearby. We wanted him to have his privacy as a young man, but we also didn't want to be too far away in case he needed us.

One of the funniest things I ever did happened when I began helping Shaquille furnish his first home in Orlando. As mothers, we don't always have the chance to do that with our children once they become adults, so I was very excited.

Oftentimes when my son moved to a new place or city, I'd help set him up in his home. One time I won't forget is when, Shaquille arranged for me to have a driver—a limo driver, that is, to get me around for my shopping. On the day that I wanted to shop for the basics for my son's home, like glasses, plates, silverware, and an iron—because he never seemed to think of getting an iron—I asked the driver to escort me to the nearest Kmart in the area. We rolled up with pride in the limo and parked the long, black car on the side of the store. I guess the limo driver was used to just waiting in the car while his patrons did whatever they had to do. But not that day! I told him to grab a cart and take one part of the store while I took the other. I'd pick the glasses and plates, while he could pick the silverware and trash cans. I'm sure that driver had no idea what his day would bring when he woke up that morning, but Kmart is ridiculously big. I needed to make the most of my day!

Along with shopping for Shaquille's house, I also organized and arranged our move from Texas to Florida, which involved enrolling the children in new schools and helping them get adapted to their different and much improved standard of living. To add to my joy, Shaquille gifted me with my first car in my own name. Who'd have thought I'd be in my midthirties before I'd own a car?

By far, the most important aspect of my son's first year was my decision to go on the road with him during the season. As a family, we'd all agreed that whenever Shaquille entered the league, I would head out on the road with him to make sure he settled in okay. This would be a huge sacrifice for us all, but we knew it was necessary. People to this day ask how the family, particularly my youngest children, handled my absence during that time. At the time they ranged from twelve to fourteen years old. I tell them I couldn't have done it if Phil had not been such a great father. Also, my other children understood why I had to accompany Shaquille. I would have done exactly the same thing for them. My oldest child may have appeared to be this big, overpowering athlete who was able to conquer anything in his sight, but all I saw was my baby, and there was no way I was leaving him to fend for himself in that big new world. I'd met many a wolf in sheep's clothing during the recruiting process, and they scared me half to death. There was no telling what they'd do to my child.

Little did I know then that in the months and years ahead, I would be the one who would receive the education of a lifetime. In fact, a lesson in "big balling and shot calling" started before Shaquille played his first game. After going most of my life barely able to make ends meet, I had a hard time believing or accepting our new financial windfall. Unfortunately, others didn't quite share my problem, and many of them spent my son's money with reckless abandon. On the other hand, I was still so plagued by worries that this dream world we'd been swept into would end somehow abruptly, that I cautioned against any large purchases Shaquille had in mind.

Shaquille has always had a good head on his shoulders for business, much like his Grandfather Hilton. He was never one to throw away his money on frivolous things, but now he was a part of a different world; a brand new fraternity of sorts, where fast living and big spending were the norm. He was also now living in the national and international spotlight, with his smiling face appearing on billboards, city buses, and T-shirts. I didn't know what effect that would have on his young, eighteen-year-old mind. Yes, I was confident in the values we'd instilled in him while he was a child, but no matter how great your parenting techniques are, outside influences can be oh-so-enticing. They are never far away, waiting for the opportunity to sneak in and take over.

One moment I still chuckle about is the day the entire family joined Shaquille at a local music store to help him pick out new stereo equipment for his home. My son has always loved music, particularly rap, so he insisted on purchasing top-notch, state-of-the-art equipment. He wanted the entire top-of-the-line equipment the store had to offer. And why shouldn't he have the chance to splurge? He'd worked tirelessly for years to get to this point, and he deserved to enjoy every minute of it. So as we browsed around the store that Friday, I watched as Shaquille pointed out a speaker here and a turntable there on the shelves to the sales associate helping him. This went on for a few hours. My son was happy as a lark, and everything was just fine and dandy, until we got to the cash register. I could tell something was very wrong by the sales clerk's ever-widening eyes as he punched in item after item.

In the end, Shaquille's purchases totaled more than ten thousand dollars, and this was back in 1992. Being the frugal woman I was and still am, I simply could not wrap my mind around such an outlandish figure for a couple of metal boxes. Something had to be done. So I decided to pull the salesclerk aside for a little "Big Lou" negotiating. I asked him if the store had a layaway plan and if he thought we'd be eligible for it. The clerk just stood there looking at me with the blankest stare I'd ever seen. In an instant,

Shaquille came over and immediately escorted me to the other side of the store, calmly explaining that he'd just signed a contract for millions of dollars and that he could well afford the music system he wanted. I think his exact words were, "Ma, let me spend my money." Here I was, still stuck in that old mind-set of deficit and fear—my son wouldn't let me stay there for long.

As it turned out, going on the road for the first year of Shaquille's NBA career would teach me a lot more about myself than it would my son. Shaquille got along just fine in this new world of flash and glitter. He'd literally turned into a man right before my eyes. I'd often sit in the stands at away games just to give him the comfort of seeing a familiar face. Fans for the opposing teams could be so cruel, hurling nasty insults toward my boy as if he were taking food out of their mouths. Ironically, I don't think those insulting comments bothered Shaquille in the least bit, but boy, did they have me seeing red. They still do. For the life of me, I have never been able to understand why so many adults get so angry about a game. What's the point of getting so irate that you then feel the need to degrade and abuse players who are just providing entertainment?

What I do know is that more than a few fans have been fortunate over the years that the Big Lou in me didn't come out while they were dissing my son. There have been several occasions where it took everything I had not to lose my temper. You'd be surprised at the nasty things people say when they *do* realize I'm Shaquille's mother. That seems to make some of the hard-core sports nuts go even crazier. My son always tells me to keep my calm at these times, because their words don't hurt him. Maybe not, but they hurt me. I admit that I've gotten better over the years, but every now and then I can't help but let Big Lou out to set a few people straight.

CHAPTER 27

"New Attitude"

Be joyful in hope, patient in affliction, faithful in prayer.

—Romans 12:12

Sadly, traveling across the country and acquiring the finer things in life did little to lessen my thirst for the bottle. If anything, it helped fuel my drinking binges, because now I could afford to buy any libation I wanted; fancy wines, exotic liquors, and good old beer were always available in our new home. And just like it was during our military days, I made sure to do all my drinking inside our home, for reasons of safety and privacy.

But even that wasn't enough to protect me the night the police came to our fine new address. I still remember it well; both Phil and I were completely plastered, and at some point we started throwing things at each other. In the heat of anger I dialed 9-1-1, but I immediately regretted it and hung up; it was too late, and within five minutes the police were there. I think I forgot where we were living at the time. In my old neighborhood in Newark, the police would take forever to get there, if they came at all, no matter how serious the incident.

Whatever Phil and I were fighting about that night stopped immediately when the police rolled up to our house. In fact, we acted as though I'd dialed 9-1-1 by complete mistake and apologized profusely to the officers. I'm not too sure the police bought into our little charade, but one of the cops did ask something that rocked me to my core. He asked if we were Shaquille O'Neal's parents and added that he knew they lived somewhere in the subdivision. Now, I was drunk, but there was no way on earth I was about to embarrass my son like that. Before Phil could part his lips, I quickly denied any relation to the center who played for the Orlando Magic. Unfortunately, I was too drunk to realize that we were probably the only black family in the neighborhood, and that pretty much gave us away.

But, what else could I do? We'd acted a straight fool that night and had potentially put Shaquille into a very difficult position that could draw lots of negative attention to him in the press and beyond. I knew I couldn't let that happen again. That very night was when I hit my rock bottom. I vowed to stop drinking for the benefit of everyone, including my son who had been so good to us and who had the most to lose. It would be one of the toughest things I'd ever have to do, but I needed the test to see if I was ready for what lay ahead. The future would demand that I have my wits about me, so staying sober was imperative.

Thankfully, there were several female role models who inspired me to step up my game across the board. While Shaquille was still in college, I had the opportunity to meet David Robinson's mother,

Linda, at a San Antonio Spurs game. I remember being very struck by her effortless polish and grace. She was like a walking textbook on confidence and style. She also had the kindest and gentlest demeanor, and she spoke in a soft and sweet voice that reminded me of my mother's. I thought to myself, *Now, that's a mother any child would be proud to have.* I always wanted to be a source of pride for my children, someone they would be happy to introduce to their friends and coworkers alike. I held on to that visual of Mrs. Robinson for years after we met to remind myself that someone was always watching, so I had to be on my best behavior always. This was not an easy task given my background, but I was determined to at least try, especially since (in my mind) there was so much to lose if I slipped up.

Something else became crystal clear to me as I traveled on the road with Shaquille during the '92–'93 NBA season. While I was out on the road for days at a time, I really missed my other children, but what I didn't miss so much was the mundane routine of my marriage. This revelation caused me a great deal of guilt as I struggled with what that feeling actually meant as we became accustomed to our new lives. I'd given so much to my marriage and the life we had together, but the disconnection I felt from my spouse just continued to widen. When I was in town, I spent my days shopping or lunching with my children or friends. I would do anything I could think of not to be in the house with Phil. Can you imagine not wanting to be in your own gorgeous, five-bedroom, eight-bathroom mansion with an elevator and a pool? I'd forever dreamed of having a home with a pool, even though I couldn't swim a lick. It just sounded glamorous. Our home was the epitome of luxury, courtesy of our son. But it wasn't enough to mask two people growing apart, even if one of those people still had no clue what was going on.

Unfortunately, I would have little time to ponder the troubled state of my marriage, because my mother's declining health suddenly became my main concern. I'd seen it before with my grandfather, an elder reluctant to share with anyone in the family that he was feeling poorly. My mother worked as a nurse for years, but she still didn't take the time to care for herself as diligently or with the same level of concern and attentiveness that she showed when she cared for others. My brother, sister, and I were so busy living our own lives with our families that we didn't see the signs, if any existed, that our mother's health was deteriorating. She'd never been one to complain. Since she rarely attended Shaquille's games (because she hated large crowds), I didn't see her as much as I would have liked to during that time. She much preferred to watch her grandson play basketball on television in the comfortable home he'd purchased and renovated for her in New Jersey.

She was ailing, and eventually she could no longer hide from her family that her health was in jeopardy. She was frequently not feeling well, had been in the hospital, and she suffered from severe stomach pains. By the time she gathered us all together in her doctor's office during the summer of 1993, she'd been diagnosed with advanced ovarian cancer. We were devastated, so much so that we were clueless about what to do next. My mother's doctor seemed competent enough, and we all agreed with his prescribed course of treatment, which included chemo and radiation. In retrospect, I wish I'd known to get a second opinion. I did not understand that there were highly regarded specialists all over the country that could have assisted my mother and help her feel more comfortable as the disease progressed. At that point, we felt she was getting the best care she could, but we knew so little about the disease or its treatment. There is far more known today about ovarian cancer, thanks to the existence of the Internet, support groups, and more government research. But we were literally baffled back then. We had no idea how to be more proactive, and beyond the obvious medical concerns we had for our mother, we all (mostly me) had to come to terms with the fact that she was fighting a losing battle.

For most of my life, my mother had been that steady presence in my life that never wavered as I fought so many demons. Even when we were torn away from her, I could still feel her presence deep inside me. She was my biggest fan and my staunchest supporter. It simply had never occurred to me that she just wouldn't be there one day, especially then, when circumstances were just beginning to look up for the entire family. But I've learned that that's the way life works sometimes; one door opens wide as another one quietly closes, sometimes forever.

For years my relationship with God had taken a backseat in my life. For most of my time as an adult, I listened to the biblical words my mother relentlessly preached, understanding little of what she was really trying to say. Without either of us knowing it, she was trying to prepare me for what was to come in my life— both the good and bad. Still, I didn't go to church, and I rarely took the time to read the Bible. But when my mother, my truest friend, became seriously ill, I ran full speed to Jesus, and He welcomed me with open arms.

This is the part of my life that I really enjoy sharing when I reach out to the many people I have a chance to meet and speak to today. So many of us wander off the path and away from the love of God, then question how we can ever find our way back to His love. But I can testify from firsthand experience that while we may drift away from the Lord, He never leaves our side. He is our parent, and He is extremely patient in His love for us. He understands that sometimes we will rebel and go our own way. But the door to His home is always open, and the locks are never changed. When I faced the reality of losing my mother, my earthly parent, I was completely lost until I took the time to realize that I have a heavenly Parent as well. Yes, my earthly father was still living, but the connection I had with my mother was unmatched. All I could do was reach back to the faith that had sustained me as a young child. This was the faith of my ancestors, my grandparents, and so many other African Americans who've been through the fire and survived. Yes, my faith was restored through the most tragic of circumstances, but remember: God welcomes us home at any time and for any reason.

CHAPTER 28

Mommy

As a mother comforts her child, so will I comfort you.

—Isaiah 66:13

As my mother's illness progressed and worsened over the next three years, the confusing state of my own life never slowed down, not even for a minute. I continued to battle a bevy of conflicting emotions about myself, my marriage, and the new world we were living in. Watching my mother fight for her life with so much quiet dignity and strength forced me to reevaluate what I wanted the next phase of my own journey to be. Would I continue to stand still, never reaching beyond what was right in front of me, or would I finally learn to love myself enough to do the things that actually made me feel fulfilled? And what exactly were those things, anyway? It would take me a good, long minute to realize that I still had absolutely no idea.

I'd spent so much of my life as a mother, as a wife, and now as the mother of a world-famous personality that I had never taken the time to learn the things that made me tick. All of my interests were vested in their interests, and their dreams became my dreams. Then, before I knew it, I was watching one of my children soar to heights few imagined and even fewer were able to realize. But, and I am slightly embarrassed to admit this, there were times when all that came to my mind was, *What about me*? It was so clear that somewhere along the way, Lucille had gone missing. I'd actually forgotten that there was a time when I had aspirations, too, and that they were still inside of me, but tucked so far down I had forgotten how to reach them. At some point I was going to have to go digging for them.

Still, I hated having those feelings of regret, even if they were only fleeting. All of my children have been the best gifts I've ever received, and I wouldn't trade the experience of being their mother for anything in the world. But feelings (just like life) are never very simple. We all fight the thoughts in our head that are better kept in silence; it's human nature.

So, I continued to mask my true thoughts about what was going on in my life, worried that others would interpret my unhappiness and thoughts as jealousy or resentment of Shaquille's success, or even worse, that they would think I was ungrateful. What I was actually feeling was so far from that. It wasn't until years later that I realized that everything going through my head was completely normal and natural. I'd been thrust into the public spotlight with little warning, and it seemed as though I had lost control of my life overnight. There was no handbook on how to handle your world being turned upside down, or even better, there certainly was no handbook entitled *The Idiot's Guide to Being an NBA Mother.* (I think I might need to write that one.) So, it was completely trial and error those first few years. And yes, there were days when I wished we could all just go back to the way we were and split a can of corned beef hash and Spam. But, trust me, those feelings didn't hang around for very long. I was living a blessed life, and I knew it.

Even as I watched my mother wither away from cancer, I continued to focus on how good God had been to our family and me. My faith was being tested, and my mind often questioned why my mother, one of the kindest and sweetest people I have ever known, had to suffer so much during the last few months of her life.

Though I had put all my faith in God, I was still very scared about what was to come if my mother died, but I couldn't let anyone know that. My siblings were all still living in New Jersey, near our mother, and working hard to take care of her every need. I wanted to leave home and be in New Jersey, too, but my mother wouldn't hear of it. I had the most children out of all of my siblings, and so everyone insisted I stay in Florida with them. Every time I'd call my mother to ask how she was and if she needed me, she'd say, "Lou, stay home with your husband and kids. I'm all right."

My siblings updated me constantly, and their stories of how our mother was so strong and full of pride that she wouldn't even let them accompany her to chemotherapy treatments left me even more in awe of her. They said she never complained about being in pain, even after the numerous surgeries she had to remove her intestines as the cancer continued to spread. She wouldn't say a word, but I could tell she was hurting. Twice a month I'd go up to New Jersey from Florida to help my sister Vivian out and sit with our mother at night. During those very still and dark hours,

I'd hear my mother's low and drawn-out moans in between her labored breathing. I could barely stop the tears from falling as I sat there feeling completely helpless.

After years of my mother guiding and comforting me through all the trying events in my life, here I was, unable to do anything to lessen her agony. With all of Shaquille's success and fame, nothing could stop life's natural course or God's plan for our lives.

My brother and sisters were such a blessing to me during this time. In a family, everyone has their own place and purpose, and those positions become crystal clear when an emergency arises. My sister, Vivian, actually moved her family into my mother's house so she could be there for her night and day. My brother, Roy, and my sister, Velma, also took turns assisting Vivian and running errands. I felt so far away in Florida, but with the kids in school and the new responsibilities I'd taken on running Shaquille's fan club and office, going up on weekends seemed like the best alternative.

Being at home in Orlando was also imperative for me for other reasons, particularly because my oldest daughter, Lateefah, really needed me. She was in her senior year of high school and struggling with some serious issues of her own. The biggest of them was an unplanned pregnancy that brought me right back down memory lane. It was as if I was reliving my own high school experience some twenty years later, and in HD.

I was determined to make the situation a lot easier for my child. How could I condemn or harshly criticize her when I'd been exactly where she was so many years ago? Phil took the news a lot harder than I did (most fathers do), and this certainly wasn't the future I wanted for our daughter either, but it was what it was. I wanted Lateefah to have the future I didn't have. I wanted her to have the chance to attend college and follow her dreams wherever they led. Somehow I'd forgotten that delayed does not mean denied. I had to remember that none of our children were in jail or strung out on drugs, and that was reason enough to be grateful. Plus, she wouldn't have the financial stress I had when Shaquille was born.

I pledged to my daughter that I would be there for her in any way I could, and that we'd all support her decision to have the baby. In an odd way, it was a welcome relief as the news about my mother's health worsened.

When you've always had babies in the house, you miss the laughter and joy they bring. I'd actually thought about adopting, since all of my children were in high school and beyond. Phil completely ignored that suggestion—as did most of my kids, who thought I had to be kidding. But I felt that we had so much to share now, and there were so many children out there in need. God was listening, and now I wouldn't have to look outside our family for a new baby to love. We'd be welcoming a new life into our home, and a whole lot of happiness right when it was sorely needed. After the birth of my first granddaughter, Shaquirah (named in honor of her uncle, Shaquille), in September, I patiently helped and taught my daughter how to warm the milk, change diapers, and cradle her daughter in the crook of her arm while holding her head straight. I also watched as Phil fell head over heels in love with our beautiful granddaughter. That baby brought us so much happiness, and she still does some fourteen years later.

By the end of that year, my mother's health had gotten to the point where the doctors gathered all of us and told us that there was simply nothing else they could do. I don't think there is anything harder for a family member to hear than those words. I feel for any person who's had to accept that a loved one will not recover, and I know there are many—far too many. It's such a hollow and numbing moment; I wouldn't wish it on my worst enemy. With the end near, I packed my bags in January of 1996 and headed to New Jersey for a long stay. I was so afraid my mother would die without me there, or that she would die alone. It was an irrational fear, considering my siblings were with her around the clock; but death, and even the prospect of it, isn't very rational.

Before my mother's illness, I would often hear people say how they prayed their loved ones would pass on so the pain and suffering would stop. I couldn't imagine feeling that way about anyone I loved until my mother's final days. I often found myself asking the Lord to spare her another day of pain and give her the peace and rest she so deserved. I know that's what she wanted too.

Being the organized and focused woman she was, she prepared us well for her death. She planned her own funeral, complete with songs, speakers, and place of burial. She left nothing to chance. All her children had to do was follow her directions. When she passed away on April 2, 1996, we respected her wishes and carried them out like little soldiers.

At her funeral, which remains the saddest day of my life, I was completely in a daze as I sat listening to her eulogy. Even though I knew the day was coming and even prayed that it would, when it finally happened, I was still in shock. Shaquille was so grief stricken at our loss that day that he punched a hole in the church's front door. I felt so bad for my son because he just couldn't understand how he could have so much and not be able to keep his grandmother alive. He struggled with that feeling many times over the years when life dealt the family numbing blows. He later had to purchase the church two new front doors.

By far, the most important instructions my mother had for our family were to stick together and to love one another without fail. She repeated that to each of us again and again before she passed, and it worked. Her illness had actually forced us to depend on each other more than ever, and now, without the main glue that held us together, we stay close to feel her presence. I often tell my brother and sisters that she told me I was in charge, as the oldest girl. Of course, they didn't hear her say it, so to this day I'm not sure they believe me.

I don't know what I would have done if I hadn't reconnected with Jesus before my mother's death. The pain of her loss is something I still feel very strongly to this day, more than ten years later. But as I tell audiences when I speak to them, it is my walk with God that's gotten me through many sleepless nights. He changed my life and made me strong where I was weak. I'm grateful to my mother for making sure I kept that connection to God. It was her will and persistence that made me realize I needed Jesus more than ever. As I mentioned earlier, today, I still keep her signature Avon perfume in my bedroom; remarkably, it still has some of its scent left. I also keep a few of her hats and other little things that remind me of her around my house. There really isn't a day that goes by when I don't think of something she said to me or something she did to make someone else's life better.

In 1996, after my mother's death, we birthed the Odessa Chambliss Quality of Life Fund, designed to award nursing students with financial scholarships. We named it "Quality of Life" because those are the words the doctor used when he said nothing more could be done for our mother. He said it was "now about the quality of life and not the quantity." Those words stuck in all of our minds, because they were so final, yet caring as well. My mother loved being a nurse so much, and we could think of no better way to celebrate her life than with a fund designed to bring more of these wonderful caregivers into the field. I'm passionate about the mission of this fund, so much so that I work in some way on it a little bit every day. It keeps me close to her memory and even closer to her goals. To date, we've raised over a million dollars for nursing students, and I couldn't be more pleased. I like to think my mother would be too.

✷

CHAPTER 29

Starting Over

So also you have sorrow now,
but I will see you again, and your hearts will rejoice,
and no one will take your joy from you.

—John 16:22 (ESV)

Nothing brings clarity to the mind and soul like the loss of someone dear. After my mother passed away, I was able to take a very long look at myself and at the decisions I had made. All the things she encouraged me to do (and not do) stayed on my mind almost all the time. "Stop being so pitiful," was her favorite thing to say to me, and God knows I was pitiful in the weeks and months following her death. It was only then that I realized something very important about my own resolve. During my mother's illness, I'd stopped drinking after some twenty years of doing so regularly. I even stopped taking my occasional puffs of Kool Filter Kings. I didn't have to join AA, although I know it's a wonderful program that helps many people; I just relied on my faith in God to get me through those nights I wanted a drink so bad I could taste the white zinfandel on my lips. Being strong enough to survive that made me realize that I was a lot stronger and more self-reliant than I knew or gave myself credit for. I'd always been plagued by the gnawing feeling that I needed something or someone as a shoulder or crutch to lean on. But as it turned out, I was pretty good at taking care of myself all along. That was a fabulous feeling to finally have.

Around this time, I also began to spread my wings by stepping out more into the Orlando social scene. I concentrated on working closely with various underserved charities. I focused on children living in lower-income communities and poor families struggling to make ends meet. This kind of work was something my son also felt compelled to do. Giving back really did my heart good for the obvious Christian reasons, but it was also good for me because during the early years of Shaquille's success, I often questioned why our family had been chosen to receive such good fortune. It was hard to understand why we had been rewarded and not the family down the street or the family on the next block. I still hadn't been able to shake that attitude of mental welfare that easily made me feel so unworthy of joy and happiness.

As I continued to get closer to God, I began to understand that there was no need for me to apologize to anyone for my family's many blessings; but it was our responsibility to share those blessings with others. Once I accepted that way of thinking, I didn't spend much time questioning why all of the good things were happening to us. Instead, I just thanked the Lord for them. I know so many of us fall into that same trap of feeling unworthy or less than adequate to receive all that God has to offer us. But how can we expect to receive God's love, mercy, and grace if we're not ready with open arms?

That epiphany also coincided with my search for a church to call home, where I could regularly worship. It had been so long since I attended weekly religious services that it turned into a much more arduous task than I thought it was going to be. It took nearly ten visits to churches all over Orlando before I found one that seemed to meet my list of needs.

At the top of my list was being able to worship and fellowship with people who saw me as Lucille O'Neal, their sister in Christ, and nothing more—not much to ask, but extremely difficult to find in this star-crazed world. Not that I considered myself a star, but even being related to one can get more attention than you'd imagine. I eventually found a little church called 910 Church of God near downtown Orlando. I love the people, and I know God meets me there every time I attend. I owe God so much, because I have been a bad girl during my life. But we serve a forgiving and loving God. Though I love to fellowship with the people in that old building, I learned that the church is not within those walls but inside of me.

By the middle of 1996, my family and I had really put down sturdy roots in Orlando, and for the first time in years, I had the chance to make a good deal of long-term friends, and not just any kind of friends, but "sister friends." For those who are not familiar with the term, sister friends are women who are almost as close as real biological sisters and give just as much support and love. My sister friends played such a pivotal role in my evolving into the woman I am today. They aided me spiritually, mentally, and emotionally. A few even helped me get on the exact path I needed to be on to make the tough decisions I'd been so afraid to make for so long.

One of those women whom I still hold close to my heart was an older lady named Dorcas Rose. Rose was a nearly eighty-year-old retired high school teacher. She was a fixture in the Orlando social scene, and I would see her out and about at event after event. We exchanged pleasantries whenever we met, but it would take a number of years before we actually bonded. Now, by this point, Shaquille had been in the league about four years, and we'd all become a bit savvier in how we chose to bring new people into our lives. The wounds were still fresh from the old and new friends in my life who constantly had their hands out. Some friends actually seemed to feel entitled to benefit from Shaquille's success. As a result, treading carefully with the unknown is something we did then and something we still do as a family today. Even as adults my children have been hurt so much by phony people. It's a wonder they can trust anyone at all these days.

The wonderful thing about Ms. Rose was that she seemed to inherently know this, and upon introducing herself to me, she explained that she wanted nothing material from me; she just wanted to link up and break bread sometimes. She even made it clear that she was financially well-off herself. God was truly all over my life, and meeting this woman at that particular point proved it even more. She knew so much about classes, courses, and schools in the area that she was able to help my daughter, Lateefah, get into college. Her spirited talks about what education could do for you no matter where you were in life eventually awakened a desire in me that had been dormant for so long: the desire to return to school. Of course, having the idea rekindled in my mind and actually registering for classes were still worlds apart. But Ms. Rose had opened the door to an idea that I wouldn't let go of just yet.

✳

CHAPTER 30

"The Wild, Wild West"

Wait for the LORD; be strong and take heart
and wait for the LORD.

—Psalm 27:14

With the thought of going back to school fresh in my mind, I even tried mentioning it in casual conversation a few times around the house. I wanted to see what reaction I'd get from the kids and, of course, Phil. The kids were supportive, but Phil said he didn't quite see the point of anyone going to college after age forty. Big surprise! Before I could really let my mind ponder the possibilities, another major shift in our family dynamic emerged.

After four years of playing with the Orlando Magic, Shaquille was traded to the Los Angeles Lakers. He'd talked to us a number of times about making the move, and we all knew that no player is guaranteed to stay with one team his entire career. And while Shaquille really loved Orlando and the fans, Los Angeles offered him a chance to explore many of the other avenues he was interested in trying in both the business and entertainment worlds.

Now, there are NBA mothers and fathers who move from city to city when their sons are traded to new teams. But we never considered that once Shaquille was headed to Los Angeles. Lateefah had settled nicely into her role as a new mother and had even enrolled in school. I was so proud of her. Both Ayesha and Jamal were thriving in high school, so uprooting them wouldn't have made much sense at all. Just as important, Shaquille was clearly a man who knew how to take care of himself in the big world around him. Phil and I still tried our best to keep our eye on the people Shaquille had in his life, and thankfully, many of the main people he employed were relatives and longtime family friends who had nothing but his best interests at heart. Nonetheless, there were always new lawyers, agents, and pitchmen angling for a way to get a little closer and lay claim to my son's potential projects and earnings.

During his first year with the Lakers, I decided I would take some time off and spend a few months in Los Angeles. I wanted to survey my son's new surroundings and get a taste of what the true Hollywood life was really like. For additional company, I brought along my little granddaughter, two-year-old Shaquirah. Her mother was in the middle of school, and this would give her a bit more time to study and enjoy the overall experience.

Those three months in Los Angeles were as eye-opening for me as the first few months I spent with Shaquille on the road his rookie season. Los Angeles was as exciting as I imagined, filled with celebrities, movie executives, and the most beautiful homes and beaches I'd ever seen. I relished the opportunity to attend the games (which were more like mini concert productions) and the chance to meet the likes of Denzel Washington and Jack Nicholson, who both had courtside tickets.

As most people know, Shaquille had his share of ups and downs in Los Angeles with the Lakers. His relationship with Kobe Bryant received constant public scrutiny. There never seemed to be a day that would go by that the media didn't add fuel to the fire with he said/he said articles. I can't say those weren't tough times for my son. He takes his job seriously and works hard at his craft—so the criticism did bother him on some level. That was a period when the media also seemed to do more than their share of damage. It was a constant stream of so many things that were untrue and hurtful. Though we'd gotten used to the media's sometimes painful ways, it still delivers a punch when it's a constant, day-to-day litany of lies and distortions. Through it all, I would talk to Shaquille about keeping the faith and not allowing the words of others to steal his joy. I knew it was a difficult time for him, but he made it through. He now looks back on that time as just another leg of his journey.

Besides enjoying the glamorous life, being more than three thousand miles away from home and Orlando finally gave me the space and distance to really think about what big move, if any, I'd tackle next in my own life. Trust me when I say it wasn't that I didn't have enough going on to occupy my time. My schedule was jam-packed with things to do at Shaquille's office and at the number of charitable organizations I'd begun to work with. Still, those things weren't enough to satisfy my desire to achieve something on my own that *was* my own. I wanted to become involved in activities or projects that required me to work from beginning to end using only my own resources. As human beings, I really believe we all have a desire on some level to see what we're made of. We all have that yearning inside to prove to ourselves that we can get by using just the wits and skills we were born with.

That's where I was in my life, and I simply couldn't ignore it any longer. I talked to Shaquille about my desire to further my education, and he insisted that I follow my heart and enroll. As he'd done with his sister Lateefah, he offered to pay for my education. His generosity was such a blessing to me. As time went on, he would pay for all of us to go to college.

Now all that was left was deciding what school I'd actually apply to. As a forty-something-year-old woman who hadn't been in a classroom in more than twenty years, I needed to make sure I enrolled in the school that had courses that catered to my demographic and the fact that I'd need to attend school in the afternoon, as I continued to run Shaquille's office and fan club during the earlier part of the day. That fan club always meant so much to Shaquille, and it still does. It was so important to him that every letter be answered in some way to show his fans how much they mean to him.

Whenever I chatted with Ms. Rose, she spoke a great deal about historically black colleges and universities. She talked a lot about their purpose and role in the community. She knew so much about school and life in general, that all I had to do was just sit with her and let the knowledge seep in. In her effort to teach me how to make the most of my position in the community, this wonderful lady planned and scheduled trips to both Bethune-Cookman and Florida A&M so that I could meet the presidents of the colleges in person. We also attended a number of the homecoming games. Little did I know then that she'd been working quietly behind the scenes on my behalf to ensure my entrance into one of those schools.

Bethune-Cookman University (it was a college then, though) actually had a continuing education program that was perfect, and so after a year or two of discussing, doubting, and deciding, I started classes in August of 1999.

Though I was completely scared to death at this new challenge in my life, those first few weeks of school were as amazing and soul satisfying as I knew they would be. That's not to say I didn't struggle, because I most certainly did. I hadn't picked up a book in nearly two decades, and I'd left half of my memory back in a beer bottle somewhere.

But I'd come too far to give up, so I worked twice as hard at my studies, constantly pushing away those nagging, negative thoughts that tried to convince me I didn't have what it took to finish. It seemed those voices screamed in my ear the loudest when I sat in my algebra classes, or any other math class for that matter. My brain simply refused to process numbers for some reason. I had one math teacher who was so patient with me that it made it all the easier. My mental-welfare attitude was slowly eroding. Thankfully, some of the students also took mercy on me, and their support helped my brain slowly but surely begin to take it all in. One of the things I think I grew to love most about returning to school was the people I ended up meeting there. I can't remember all the names of the many students who offered to assist me while I adapted again to school life. Their kindness just reinforced my faith in God and in His goodness. He steered just the right people in my direction during that time to help me fulfill my dream.

Eventually, school would become so overwhelming that I would give up working in my office on Shaquille's fan mail so that I could focus full-time on my studies. After my second year of school, I transferred to the main campus in Daytona Beach with the regular students. That meant I'd be taking classes with kids my own children's ages, but I had no fear or worries by that time. Yes, I felt a bit older, but my confidence had begun to soar with every class I took and passed with flying colors. And nothing made my day better than when of one the kids on campus found out whose mother I was. As I walked to class on campus, I could hear them attempt to whisper, "Hey, that's Shaq's mom."

In time and without fail, those same students would say to me, "Ms. Lucille, aren't you rich? Why are you even in school?" By the time I explained my reasons, I'm sure those students were very sorry they asked. But I had to impress upon them that knowledge and information had little to do with money or fame. I would tell them that all the money in the world won't help if you don't have the smarts and intelligence to go with it. "How are you going to manage your money if you can't count or read the fine print of a contract?" I could see the lightbulbs go off in a few of their faces with my words, while others still seemed utterly confused. But what I loved most about those conversations with the kids was that I felt like I was really fitting in with their world and giving them a dose of reality that they sorely needed.

There are many days when I wish I could return to school and sit in a few classes, just to give students that same speech about the need for knowledge. In today's world, getting a higher education is a privilege that ever fewer people are able to afford as costs climb sky high. Our children need to understand what a gift having that opportunity is to them and their future. I would tell them the same thing I tell my own children—that opportunity only comes so often, and you must be ready to reach out and grab it when it does. Sure, many have heard that same piece of advice a million times over, but it doesn't make it any less true. I've seen far too many people miss an opportunity that never comes around again.

All those years of self-doubt and self-pity that crippled me began to crumble bit by bit as I looked toward a future with fewer and fewer limitations. If anyone had told me ten years before that I'd be working on my degree, I would have laughed in their face. I never saw the possibility of changing my life while struggling to figure out how to feed a family of six with one chicken. But that is the true beauty of God's plan for us. We may not know what His plans hold for us, but we must trust that they are bigger and better than anything we could ever imagine for ourselves.

With God all things are possible.

—Matthew 19:26 (NKJV)

CHAPTER 31

"Through the Fire"

Call upon me in the day of trouble; I will deliver you,
and you will honor me.

—Psalm 50:15

I began the year 2001 feeling truly at peace with where I was headed in my life, for the first time in years. I was in college and doing quite well in my classes, with nearly a 4.0 average. I'd developed quite a nice circle of friends whom I could depend on, and my children seemed to be thriving in their own lives as well. That's probably why I took more than a few people by surprise when I filed for divorce from Phil in February of that year. No one on the outside looking in had a clue that we were having problems. I'd kept my feelings of discontent with my personal life to myself for more than twenty years; it was private, and I wanted to keep it that way. Not that holding it all on the inside did my health any favors. My hair had fallen out in spots, and I was often nervous and anxious for no apparent reason. But deep down, I knew why. For years I'd been very unhappy with my marriage and Phil's sometimes controlling nature, but I held on out of fear of the unknown. How would I fare alone in the world when I'd been married since I was nineteen years old?

Like so many women, I was afraid that I wouldn't be able to care for myself or make the tough decisions I needed to make to live life on my own. And like many women, I wanted my children to grow up in a home with two parents. I never had that, and I didn't and wouldn't deny them that chance. So I put my happiness on the back burner and waited for God to give a sign when the time was right for me to leave my marriage.

After Shaquille entered the NBA and worries about money and basic survival lessened, I finally took the time to really think about what I needed from my life and what direction I wanted the next phase of it to go in. College was definitely a destination on the path, but while I was enjoying attending school full-time, I knew there was still something missing, and that something had been missing for a long time. There was a seemingly endless void that appeared to grow even deeper with each passing year.

That kind of emptiness shouldn't have been there after twenty-eight years of marriage. Phil and I were, in a sense, living two different lives in the same house, and as far as I was concerned, it no longer made sense for that to continue. Phil, however, didn't feel the same way, and I know he didn't want a divorce, but I finally had to do what was right for me.

I assured my friends and family that I hadn't made the decision in haste, so I had no regrets, though I was sorry that Phil was angry and hurt about my decision. I'd actually thought about leaving my marriage off and on for years. But it wasn't until I discussed it with my children, and ultimately with God, that I knew the time was right. All my children, including Shaquille, are still very close to their father, and I support that. I did what I could to make sure that nothing I did changed my children's relationships with him. I do think it was hard on each of them to see their parents apart. But they all understood it needed to happen. Shaquille was very supportive, particularly since he'd heard me speak of leaving a number of times. One day he just asked me not to talk about it anymore and "do it."

On the same morning I filed the divorce papers with my lawyer, I moved out of the million-dollar mansion Phil and I had shared for ten years. I left quite a few things behind that day, including a little of myself. I left material things, like trophies, gifts, and pictures, but I'd made peace with leaving those random objects where they were. That's what I needed and had to do in order to move forward. Many of my friends still can't believe I left so much behind, but I considered it a fair trade-off for my personal joy. I know many women out there have been in the same position. After you've worked so hard and so long for something, how can you just leave it behind? But I say, what's the use of having all the clothes, shoes, and jewelry in the world if you're not happy? I worried quite a bit about starting over with nothing. Yes, I had a wealthy son, but I pledged to myself that I would never be dependent on him. He loves to purchase me fabulous gifts and beautiful trinkets, but he does these things because he wants to—not because I ask. I feel exactly the same way today. I've never been one to place much value on fancy or material things. I'd prefer that Shaquille save his money and spend it on himself and his family. I'm a simple woman with simple tastes, and as the Los

Angeles–based bishop Noel Jones is fond of saying in his sermons, "you don't take old furniture to a new house." I couldn't agree more. I also left my married name (Harrison) behind and returned to Lucille O'Neal. I'm sure that raised a few eyebrows, but in reality I was attempting to reclaim the "me" that I'd lost so many years ago. Continuing to use my married name would have defeated that purpose. I left that union and the name as well.

After I moved out, I'd found a quaint, three-bedroom, one-floor home that I loved. It was just big enough for me and some little knickknacks I kept for myself. I called it my "little hut" (and still do), and oh, how I just enjoyed the sense of calm, relaxation, and freedom I felt every time I walked through the door. As corny as it might sound, freedom was something I'd been craving for a very long time. I relished the freedom to think for myself, do for myself, and just be myself without ever looking over my shoulder for approval and validation. I could finally leave my room junky, the dishes out overnight without washing them, or my shoes smack-dab in the middle of the bedroom floor without giving it another thought. That's freedom for you. I felt completely reborn! I still do a little dance in the hallway of my hut to express my joy.

But, just when you're not looking, life has a way of throwing yet another curveball. Soon after our separation, my youngest daughter, Ayesha, began to complain that she was having strange pains in her ear, throat, and the entire right side of her face. I'd always called Ayesha my miracle baby because she'd been born prematurely, but she flourished quite beautifully as a child and as an adult. When the pain persisted, I encouraged my baby girl to go see a doctor because I was baffled by her symptoms. For months the doctors told her it was just a cold or an ear infection, or that her jaw was out of alignment. They would just prescribe her antibiotic after antibiotic and send her home to deal with the throbbing pain on her own. Often, the pain would subside for a period, only to come back in a few weeks, with a vengeance. No doubt frustrated, Ayesha just stopped complaining altogether after a while.

That June, my family was on top of the world as Shaquille celebrated winning the 2001 NBA championship with the Lakers. Ayesha and I flew to Los Angeles to celebrate with Shaquille and to spend some quality time with him. Unfortunately, Ayesha was still having health issues, and when she told her brother about it, he immediately connected her with a few of the best local doctors he knew in the Los Angeles area. We all just wanted her to feel better. She made the doctor's appointment for the day of the Lakers' victory parade, and though I didn't go to the parade, I didn't accompany Ayesha to the doctor, either; how I regretted that decision.

CHAPTER 32

Another Test

Surely the arm of the LORD is not too short to save,

nor his ear too dull to hear.

—Isaiah 59:1

On a day that should have been one of the happiest in our lives, Ayesha was being told she had suspicious fluid in the area where her ear was aching. I had initially dismissed the pain she was feeling as something minor, but hearing her say there was fluid behind her ear made my stomach immediately drop. I feared the absolute worst, and I was so upset that I hadn't been there to hold her hand at the doctor's office when she was told the news. Though I didn't dare say it, I knew that she was seriously ill, and I all could do was wonder how we'd survive it.

I fell to my knees and cried out to the Lord, "Please let my baby be okay." I'd watched my mother suffer for years in illness, and I couldn't bear to think about my daughter going through the same ordeal. My faith was being tested yet again, but I knew that I needed to rely on it now more than ever. I'd learned years before to give every situation I faced to God and then let go. But that can be so hard to do, to sit back and allow God to do His work on His time. Often, we want to take matters into our own hands, when ultimately we have absolutely no control. On the days that I would forget this, I frequently repeated the phrase "Faith without works is just like not believing." I had to believe that all would be okay. Ayesha had to believe it too. I also began to sing to my daughter every day to keep her spirits up; I would hum the words "We've come this far by faith, leaning on the Lord. Trusting in His Holy Word, He never failed me yet." I sang that song for both of us as we waited for a diagnosis.

On July 9, 2001, I watched as my twenty-two-year-old baby daughter was wheeled into the operating room at a Florida hospital to remove a cancerous tumor from her neck. At the sight of her on that gurney, an amazing calm just washed all over me, and I had to smile. A vision came to me of God holding Ayesha in His arms and guiding the surgeon's hands who was set to perform her delicate surgery. Thank You, Jesus, the operation was a success!

The surgery was only the beginning of Ayesha's harrowing journey. After the tumor was removed, she began receiving radiation treatments twice a day for over a month. All I could do was pray to God to give me the strength to hold her hand through every treatment, particularly when she was so sick she could barely hold her head up. God knows if I could have traded places with my child so that I could have been the one to go through that pain, I surely would have. "Why not make me sick instead, Lord?" I asked. What parent wouldn't want to spare their child the suffering life can often bring? Watching her endure radiation broke my heart and brought back those same feelings of helplessness I felt so many years ago with my mother. My mind would wander to the unthinkable. Was God punishing me for the many mistakes and sins I'd made over the years? Had my drinking and smoking caused my baby to be ill? Was this the way I would have to pay for my mistakes? The list of things that I'd done in my life and felt contrition about just grew longer and longer as I sat in the hospital, waiting for Ayesha to be treated.

In the daylight hours I tried to mask my fears and be strong, because I couldn't let Ayesha see me cry. I couldn't break down in front of her, because she was depending on me to get her through this ordeal, and I was all she had. To make her feel better when she lost all of her hair, I'd rub soothing oils on her scalp while promising her that it would grow back with no problem. When night came and I was alone, I shed many a tear, asking for God's mercy and His grace. I held Ayesha each day and just continued to reassure her that God was still in the miracle-working business. Yes, there were indeed times when I wanted to scream at the top of my lungs and ask, "God, why my baby and not me?" But those moments would be fleeting. I ultimately believed that God was the great Healer and the outcome would be favorable.

In God, whose word I praise, in God I trust;
I will not be not afraid.

—Psalm 56:4

Over the next few months, and as my baby tried to heal, I put my life and all my activities on hold while I focused solely on Ayesha.

Her health and well-being were all that mattered at that time, and I knew I could get her back on track and healthy with love and prayer. Oh, there were rough days and seemingly never-ending nights that I spent by her side as she tried to not only physically get better, but emotionally survive as well. Cancer is such a cruel and heartless disease that affects countless people each day. It affects the young and old, the rich and poor, and being around those suffering from it can either remind you of the brevity of life or force you to make each day even more worthwhile. For me it did both.

Only God could have brought me through the devastating news that one of my children had being stricken with a life-threatening disease at the same time my marriage was ending. But I knew if I could just be still and quiet, God would speak to me.

If everyone took time during the day to pause, we'd hear God leading and directing our paths with His small but still voice. Watching my baby regain her health was one of the best gifts God has ever given to my family and me. Ayesha has fought all her life, and just as she fought to stay alive as a baby, she'd fought as a young adult and won. She's a warrior in every way.

The year 2001 was certainly one of the toughest I faced. We as a family were shaken to our core with Ayesha's illness, on top of the reality that Phil and I had separated. In the midst of her illness, I could have halted the divorce proceedings, but I was literally suffocating in the life I had and could wait no longer to move on to the next phase of my journey. Change, really major change, is never easy. It's often uncomfortable and sad. Divorce is never easy either, since it marks the end of a union and partnership that was entered into for a lifetime. But some changes are necessary or our lives become stagnant and unfulfilling, and I refused to live that way any longer. I did mourn the loss of my marriage and the sadness I knew my children felt with their parents going their separate ways. It was also difficult for me because, to some extent, I missed Phil. In a way, we'd grown up together, and I'd spent most of my adult life with him. I loved him, but I was no longer in love with him.

With my baby back on her feet, I turned back to my studies. As I inched closer to graduation, I had to spend more time studying. I'd chosen business administration as my major, and boy, did some of those classes (statistics) cause my brain to just freeze. I would often stay up half the night, studying and preparing presentations for class the next day. During those days, I often felt like a teenager any time my friends called to go out and I'd have to say no because of homework. I took my schoolwork seriously, and I had every intention of graduating with honors, or somewhere close to it.

By March of 2002, my divorce was final, and I was able to breathe a sigh of relief. I remember doing a two-step when I received the papers. But yet again, it wasn't long before I was hit with another emotional setback when my father suddenly died. He was living in South Carolina in a small apartment near my sister, Vivian, who looked after him as she'd done with my mother. He had been fighting numerous health issues over the years and was suffering from diabetes. One day, when he didn't show up for his dialysis, family friends went to his house and found him dead in his apartment. He died alone in his bed, and that's an image that still haunts me to this day. I don't think anyone should die alone, and certainly not someone you love. With his passing, memories of the years I'd spent with my father just came raining down on me nonstop. We had such a complicated relationship in large part because he never was a father in the traditional sense. His speech impediment made our communication difficult, and the fact that we lived with his parents circumvented his authority over us. But I never doubted his love.

A few years earlier, my father had come to live with me for three months while he received radiation treatment for throat cancer at an Orlando hospital. Those months were so special to me because my father became my shadow. He'd come with me to work, help me stuff envelopes, and he would basically follow me everywhere and anywhere I had to go. I felt such a special bond with him during that period, even though he rarely spoke a word. There is no doubt that I would have preferred my father to be more of the parental figure I needed growing up. But he could only do and be what he was. It was unfair for me to expect more. It took me a while to understand that, but what a wonderful feeling it was to finally get there.

I've never been one of those people who blamed my parents for all of my life's ills, although I know that's a popular thing for people to do these days. My motto is, once you turn thirty-five years old, you need to forgive your parents for everything and let it go. I know my mother and father did the best they could raising, my brother, my sisters and me, and I honor them for that to this day.

CHAPTER 33

"Never Would Have Made It"

Blessed is the man who fears the LORD. Who delights
greatly in His commandments.

—Psalm 112:1 (NKJV)

God certainly never promised us days without rain or days
without trials and tribulations. There's no doubt in my mind
that I've had more than my share of both. I am a strong believer
that the storms in my life, or in some cases the hurricanes, have me
so very humble and grateful for where I find myself today. There
are afternoons where I do nothing but sit on the backyard terrace
of my little hut and stare at the manicured lawn while inhaling
the fragrance of freshly cut grass. I often just sit there and cast
my eyes on the colorful butterflies as they dance and flutter all
around the yard. These are the moments I truly savor because I
feel so at peace with nature, and most important, it is during these
moments that I feel at one with God.

At nearly fifty-six years old, I can honestly say that I'm the happiest and most satisfied I've ever been with myself and with my life. As women, we are so often led to believe—through magazines, movies, and TV shows—that life ends after forty. They try to make us believe that once we reach that milestone, we cease to exist if we have a wrinkled forehead, sagging anything, or no man to speak of. I'm a living and breathing testament that life begins and flourishes at whatever age you become comfortable in your own skin and whenever it is that you fall in love with what you see when you look in the mirror each morning.

The day I graduated with my college degree in business administration opened a floodgate of joy that continues to flow inside of me even today. I remember having a permanent smile on my face the entire afternoon of my graduation. I was floating on air before the ceremony. I had been elected class secretary by my classmates, which afforded me the opportunity to represent the summer class of graduates.

Bethune-Cookman College—now a university—presents Lucille O'Neal, graduate, bachelor of science–business administration, class of 2003. I have learned that I have all I need within me to accomplish my goals. What an experience!

It also meant that I was the one who was to place a wreath on the grave of Dr. Mary McLeod Bethune (the founder of the college) before the graduation. Can you imagine the honor of being able to salute such an amazing woman? She had been such an inspiration to me because of her story. She was the child of slaves and went on to become a college graduate during the late 1800s. This was an accomplishment unheard-of during that time for an African American, but especially for an African-American woman. She fought through so much adversity until she received the education she had dreamed of. Sound familiar? She later became an advisor to President Franklin D. Roosevelt, and was one of the first black female college presidents in the country.

On that day in 2003, I'd accomplished something on my own that had taken a great deal of blood, sweat, and tears, and no one could ever take it away from me. There is no better feeling than that. The words my mother used to say to me echoed in my ears, and they still do. She often said, "Everything you have to work for should be worth having." No truer words have ever been spoken.

In the years since my divorce, my daughter's illness, and my college graduation from Bethune-Cookman University, I've ventured even further outside of my comfort zone by accepting numerous invitations I have received from groups and organizations wanting me to speak each year. As a child, I'd dreamed of becoming a public speaker. The idea of mere words having the capacity to influence people to act, move, or react to information (and get paid for it, too) still amazes me to this day.

Watching President Barack Obama skillfully command audiences with his inspiring oration during his historic campaign was true proof of what words can do to uplift and give people hope. In her own way, my earliest mentor, Rev. Hartsfield, was my Barack Obama. The sway she had over her congregation was what first taught me the potency of the spoken word, and I've longed to have that kind of verbal command ever since.

Fortunately, I've had the chance to experiment with my vocal discourse in a variety of smaller arenas, such as with the group Mothers of Professional Basketball Players. I was one of the twenty-three mothers who started the organization years ago. This group of other mothers and I founded the group in an effort to give mothers support after their sons entered into the league. It can be an altogether staggering ordeal for any parent, and I, for one, felt it was imperative for those of us with experience to offer assistance to any family in need.

Even before my divorce, I was the secretary of the group, and I found myself working with the organization quite regularly. I was also very close to the president, Charlotte Brandon. I helped to organize our conventions, fund-raisers, and other activities for the mothers during the conference, and I frequently spoke to the group about my experiences as a parent of a high-profile player.

Being able to converse with other women with similar situations did wonders for my soul, and the opportunity to speak out loud in front of these women, who were also friends, gave me the comfort I needed to perfect my voice and message. It's an amazing sensation to know that you're giving someone in need a shoulder to lean on and an ear to listen. In our regular meetings and annual conventions, we discuss everything from the security we feel our sons need to the way the media portrays them. Younger mothers often question older mothers about money issues, groupies, and the toll of injuries on the family. I feel so good that this was started, because so many families feel out of sorts when this wonderful/confusing world happens upon them. We all needed a way to get that information to one another and rely on each other's strength.

Today, I'm the elected president of the organization. It's a position that requires me to be available at all times for new mothers who are often overwhelmed and baffled by their new roles and lives. With a son who's been in the league and in the spotlight for close to eighteen seasons, I'm uniquely qualified to answer more than a few questions on the topic. These women also give me another support system to depend on when times get rough, and for that I'm truly grateful. As a group, we've seen each other through illness, divorce, and even the death of some of our members. Because we have been through so much together, we've all become stronger and closer as a result.

The years of speaking with those mothers did a great deal to prepare me for the life I'm currently living. With the groups and organizations I talk to today, I often discuss having a can-do attitude. I really love discussing that topic with young women on the verge of adulthood. Many girls of their generation are too young to have developed a relationship with God; therefore I'm cautious about how deeply I touch on religion. I do broach the subject of God, with hopes of piquing their interest. What's most important to me is that they know they shouldn't doubt God or their own abilities. It is important for me to talk to them about this because I doubted both for so long, and I lost a lot of valuable time questioning my self-worth. What a waste of God's precious gift of life. If I am able to prevent just one young person from having to spend any of her precious life wondering if she matters, I will have done my job.

In most of my speeches, I ask these young women not to look

for the easy way out of situations, but to depend on God. I tell them that He will help you hold up under the pressures of life's disappointments. "'Don't worry about anything,'" I'll quote. "'Instead, pray about everything'" (Philippians 4:6 NLT). I try to let them know that I was where many of them are right now: down and out, with no idea what to do next. I try to share with them that it was only when I finally grew up enough to let God into my life that my entire world changed. When that happens, you feel compelled to tell anyone who'll listen.

These days, when I go to bed at night, I sleep on the sheets of satisfaction, the pillows of peace, and the cushions of confidence; it's better than a sleep number bed!

The joy that sharing my experiences with others (the young and the old) has brought me has been the most fulfilling part of my journey, and it continues to keep my days quite active. I am rich in so many ways that have nothing to do with money, which only serves to explain the happiness I have regarding my mental wealth today. My new life has also given me the opportunity to interact with a number of fascinating new people who have brought an entirely new perspective to my mind and my outlook. Ironically, many of those people have been of the opposite sex, and I can say with complete honesty that I've enjoyed a very spirited social life in recent years.

After twenty-eight years of marriage, I wasn't sure if I'd ever be ready for another personal relationship with a man. I had waited and fought so long to finally have my own place and space that the thought of sharing it again didn't exactly make me want to do cartwheels. Still, I don't think we're meant to be alone in this life.

The difference between now and twenty-eight years ago is that at this age I know what love is and what it isn't. I know exactly how I need it to be expressed and showcased for me to be happy. With two daughters (one recently married), I spend a lot of time talking with them about what to look for in a life partner and how important it is that they find someone who at least shares some of their interests, ideals, and morals. I've told my sons this as well.

What's even more wonderful about the last few years up to now is that I know I'm a vibrant, beautiful, and passionate woman who deserves the attention of a man who appreciates me. I finally let go of that less-than-worthy attitude. I'm the gem, the reward, and the prize, and any man out there who doesn't realize this might as well keep on going. Don't get me wrong; I know that dating is no walk in the park, especially when you haven't been out there for a while. I'd been married for so long that I had forgotten about all the little games that people play in the early stages of getting to know someone—and yes, much to my surprise, very grown men play games too. Somehow, I'd erased that part of my memory about relationships taking work—a lot of work. Go figure!

As I was beginning to navigate the maze that is the dating world, back in 2003, Shaquille began to talk about his desire to return to school to get his master's degree. Just as he had promised me, he'd completed his undergraduate education, and now he was interested in going a step further by attaining a master's degree in business.

For some odd reason, Shaquille's talk of returning to school made me once again long for the days when I stayed up all night, working on presentations and completing homework after homework assignment. Crazy, I know. But my oldest son has always had the ability to encourage me to do things I never would have thought about doing if not for him. In fact, Shaquille, Ayesha (my miracle baby), and I all pursued and received our master's degrees at the University of Phoenix in 2005, 2006, and 2007. Both of them graduated with a master's in business administration. By the grace of God, I received a master's degree in organizational management from the University of Phoenix in June of 2005. Praise the Lord, praise the Lord! What a blessing! I promise you, I am using everything I learned in my daily life.

University of Phoenix, graduating class of 2005, master's of organizational management. This old girl has some great initials behind her name now . . . Lucille O'Neal, BS, MOM. I know I never could have made it without God on my side!

Even though there seems to be an endless amount of hustle and bustle in my life, I can assure you that there is no relationship that I focus on more than the one I have with God. I'm not trying to be perfect or holier-than-thou; it's just that I owe God my life. After so many years of not giving Him my full and undivided attention, I now do what I can to serve and honor Him at all times. This makes me a true servant, and I love it. I work as the office manager in my church, which is truly an assignment from God. I also attend two church services each Sunday when I am not traveling. I do this because I know that without God's grace and mercy over my life, I never would have made it this far. With God at the center of my life, I continue to be content with who I am and where I am. Whether or not I marry again or even get involved in another serious relationship, I know that I am not lonely and I'm not alone. When you see me walking, know that I'm about my Father's business and working for His purpose. I have my loving family, my special and true friends, and I have my God—I'm truly walking like I have somewhere to go, and I do. He gives me all the direction I need.

My children and me on my birthday in July 2006. The gang's all here . . . (left to right) Lateefah, Ayesha, Shaquille, me, and Jamal.

❊

The Lord Has Brought Me
a Mighty Long Way...

Forty is the number representing a very long period of testing and trials. I think of Moses and the Israelites in the wilderness for forty years, complaining over and over again.

When I was active in the church on a regular basis more than forty years ago, I can remember the wonderful feeling I had when the Spirit of God overwhelmed me on many occasions. The anointing was evident and burned deep inside of me! Praise God.

Somewhere I got disconnected, and it has taken me the last forty years to get back to this special place—back into an intimate relationship with God—reconnected.

I've been through tests and trials, suffered losses, been used and abused; however, through all of this, God never left me. Right now I love Him more with each dawning of a new day. I'm so grateful that God continued to love me in spite of my own imperfections. Let me share forty memorable Scriptures that helped me during my wilderness experience over the last forty plus years, and a little of what I learned in the process. God is so good.

1. Deuteronomy 8:2—"Remember how the LORD your God led you all the way in the desert these forty years, to humble you and to test you in order to know what was in your heart, whether or not you would keep his commands." *I won't complain.*

2. Psalm 119:105—"Your word is a lamp to my feet and a light for my path." *I am guided by the Word on a daily basis.*

3. Romans 8:28—"We know that in all things God works for the good of those who love him, who have been called according to his purpose." *In every circumstance learn to glorify God.*

4. Romans 1:11–12—"I long to see you so that I may impart to you some spiritual gift to make you strong—that is, that you and I may be mutually encouraged by each other's faith." *I learned to be careful of the people I connect myself to. There is power in the connection. Encourage one another and lift each other up. Speak about those things that are not, as though they were, and you could increase your faith. This attitude is catching.*

5. Ephesians 2:8—"For it is by grace you have been saved, through faith—and this not from yourselves, it is the gift of God." *What a wonderful gift! Grace is given to all of us.*

6. 1 Corinthians 10:13—"No temptation has seized you except what is common to man. And God is faithful; he will not let you be tempted beyond what you can bear. But when you are tempted, he will also provide a way out so that you can stand

up under it." *There is no situation we can get into that God will not get us out of. I've put myself in many messes with the choices I've made! Beware of various temptations.*

7. Romans 12:2—"Do not conform any longer to the pattern of this world, but be transformed by the renewing of your mind. Then you will be able to test and approve what God's will is—His good, pleasing and perfect will." *Expect an attitude adjustment that will change your way to God's way.*

8. James 4:7—"Submit yourselves, then, to God. Resist the devil and he will flee from you." *Get into the habit of saying no to wrongdoing, no to deceit, no to lying, and no to evil. Put yourself in a place to be blessed! Turn your back on anything that allows you to turn your back on God—look forward and stay focused!*

9. Proverbs 3: 5–6—"Trust in the LORD with all thine heart; and lean not unto thine own understanding. In all thy ways acknowledge him, and he shall direct thy paths" (KJV). *Don't worry about anything, but put your trust in God. In life you will experience many ups and downs. Know that God is trustworthy and you can totally depend on Him to take you where you really want to go—higher!*

10. Philippians 3:13–14—"Brothers, I do not consider myself yet to have taken hold of it. But one thing I do: Forgetting what is behind and straining toward what is ahead, I press on toward the goal to win the prize for which God has called me heavenward in Christ Jesus."

11. Philippians 4:11–13—"I am not saying this because I am in need, for I have learned to be content whatever the circumstances. I know what it is to be in need, and I know what it is to have plenty. I have learned the secret of being content in

any and every situation, whether well fed or hungry, whether living in plenty or in want. I can do everything through [Christ] who gives me strength." *Yes, I can.*

12. Matthew 25:40—"I tell you the truth, whatever you did for . . . the least of these . . . you did for me." *Make a true effort to help the needy, with love. Begin to see Jesus in every person you meet on life's journey.*

13. Psalm 37:4—"Delight yourself in the LORD and he will give you the desires of your heart." *Trust Him, let Him order your steps. Be patient and thank God for what He has done! Take pleasure in doing everything God's way as you experience peace, joy, and happiness.*

14. Matthew 28:19–20—"Therefore go and make disciples of all nations, baptizing them in the name of the Father and of the Son and of the Holy Spirit, and teaching them to obey everything I have commanded you. And surely I am with you always, to the very end of the age." *The Great Commission is a demonstration and an outline for all of us who believe. Make it a point to lead others to Christ, and help them to know and see the goodness of God in their lives as well as in your own.*

15. John 3:16—"For God so loved the world, that he gave his only begotten Son, that whosoever believeth in him should not perish, but have everlasting life" (KJV). *If God gave His all, I can't see how I could give enough now. He loved us enough to give us life—eternally!*

16. Romans 5: 3–4—"Not only so, but we also rejoice in our sufferings, because we know that suffering produces perseverance; perseverance, character; and character, hope." *I've certainly*

learned to praise God through the storms. I've come out stronger and wiser during the process as my character was built.

17. Ephesians 6:11–12—"Put on the full armor of God so that you can take your stand against the devil's schemes. For our struggle is not against flesh and blood, but against the rulers, against the authorities, against the powers of this dark world, and against the spiritual forces of evil in the heavenly realms." *Stand firm with truth, righteousness, peace, and the protection of God's Word! Evil is all around us, and we will face a battle time after time.*

18. Hebrews 11:1—"Faith is the substance of things hoped for, the evidence of things not seen" (KJV). *Believe, perceive, hear, and trust!*

19. Romans 10:9–10—"If you confess with your mouth that Jesus is Lord and believe in your heart that God raised him from the dead, you will be saved. For it is by believing in your heart that you are made right with God, and it is by confessing with your mouth that you are saved" (NLT). *Make a personal confession today—declare with your mouth, "I am saved."*

20. Psalm 118:29—"Give thanks to the LORD, for he is good; his love endures forever." *I'm grateful for each and every blessing. He has made me a woman who is: admirable, bold, courageous, destined for greatness, extraordinary, focused, good, holy, inspiring, joyful, knowledgeable, loving, magnificent, nice, optimistic, poised, qualified, righteous, steadfast, thoughtful, unmovable, vivacious, worthy, not a xerox copy of anyone, young at heart, and full of zeal and warmth.*

21. Isaiah 54:17—"No weapon . . . formed against thee shall prosper" (KJV). *This does not say that it will not form and present itself; however, it will not succeed.*

22. Psalm 121:1–2—"I will lift up mine eyes unto the hills, from whence cometh my help. My help cometh from the LORD, which made heaven and earth" (KJV). *I've learned that God is the true source of my strength, and I look up and hold on to keep God's attention.*

23. Psalm 27:1–2—"The LORD is my light and my salvation—whom shall I fear? The LORD is the stronghold of my life—of whom shall I be afraid?" *No one!*

24. Jeremiah 29:11—"'For surely I know the plans I have for you,' says the LORD, 'plans . . . to give you a future with hope'" (NRSV). *Remember the pathway . . .*

25. 2 Corinthians 12:9–10—"But he said to me, 'My grace is sufficient for you, for my power is made perfect in weakness.' Therefore I will boast all the more gladly about my weaknesses, so that Christ's power may rest on me. That is why, for Christ's sake, I delight in weaknesses, in insults, in hardships, in persecutions, in difficulties. For when I am weak, then I am strong." *There is nothing anybody can say or do that will hurt me anymore. I have been through some storms and rain . . .*

26. Lamentations 3:21–23—"Yet this I call to mind and therefore I have hope. Because of the LORD's great love we are not consumed, for his compassions never fail. They are new every morning; great is your faithfulness." *Worry is a waste of time and can become a way of life if we are not careful!*

27. Psalm 128:1—"Blessed are all who fear the LORD, who walk in his ways."

28. Proverbs 16:3—"Commit to the LORD whatever you do, and your plans will succeed." *We often wrestle with our mind and emotions—we need to stay focused on God.*

29. Psalm 19:14—"Let the words of my mouth, and the meditation of my heart, be acceptable in thy sight, O LORD, my strength, and my redeemer" (KJV). *Amen.*

30. Romans 12:9—"Love must be sincere. Hate what is evil; cling to what is good." *If it is not sincere, surely it is not L-O-V-E. A sincere person is loving, patient, prayerful, generous, kind, a true servant, etc.*

31. Proverbs 21:21—"He who pursues righteousness and love finds life, prosperity and honor." *I want to be whole and 100 percent pure, like Ivory Soap!*

32. 1 Peter 1:14–15—"As obedient children, do not conform to the evil desires you had when you lived in ignorance. But just as he who called you is holy, so be holy in all you do." *And we really can.*

33. 1 Thessalonians 5:16–18—"Be joyful always; pray continually; give thanks in all circumstances, for this is God's will for you in Christ Jesus." *I have learned to rejoice, pray, and continually thank God!*

34. James 1:2–8—"Consider it pure joy, my brothers, whenever you face trials of many kinds, because you know that the testing of your faith develops perseverance. Perseverance must finish its work so that you may be mature and complete, not lacking anything. If any of you lacks wisdom, he should ask God, who gives generously to all without finding fault, and it will be given to him. But when he asks, he must believe and not doubt, because he who doubts is like a wave of the

sea, blown and tossed by the wind. That man should not think he will receive anything from the Lord; he is a double-minded man, unstable in all he does." *Don't be double-minded when you ask God!*

35. Matthew 5:37—"Simply let your 'Yes' be 'Yes,' and your 'No,' 'No'; anything beyond this comes from the evil one." *Say what you mean and mean what you say!*

36. Psalm 107:1—"Give thanks to the LORD, for he is good; His love endures forever." *I should know.*

37. Psalm 1:1–6—"Blessed is the man who walketh not in the counsel of the ungodly, nor standeth in the way of sinners, nor sitteth in the seat of the scornful. But his delight is in the law of the LORD; and in his law doth he meditate day and night. And he shall be like a tree planted by the rivers of water, that bringeth forth his fruit in his season; his leaf also shall not wither; and whatsoever he doeth shall prosper. The ungodly are not so: but are like the chaff which the wind driveth away. Therefore the ungodly shall not stand in the judgment, nor sinners in the congregation of the righteousness. For the LORD knoweth the way of the righteous: but the way of the ungodly shall perish" (KJV). *Believe it.*

38. Psalm 23:1–6—"The LORD is my shepherd, I shall not be in want. He makes me lie down in green pastures, he leads me beside quiet waters, he restores my soul. He guides me in paths of righteousness for his name's sake. Even though I walk through the valley of the shadow of death, I will fear no evil, for you are with me; your rod and your staff, they comfort me. You prepare a table before me in the presence of my enemies. You anoint my head with oil; my cup overflows.

Surely goodness and love will follow me all the days of my life, and I will dwell in the house of the LORD forever." *Hallelujah!!*

39. Matthew 5:3–12—"Blessed are the poor in spirit, for theirs is the kingdom of heaven. Blessed are those who mourn, for they will be comforted. Blessed are the meek, for they will inherit the earth. Blessed are those who hunger and thirst for righteousness, for they will be filled. Blessed are the merciful, for they will be shown mercy. Blessed are the pure in heart, for they will see God. Blessed are the peacemakers, for they will be called [the children] of God. Blessed are those who are persecuted because of righteousness, for theirs is the kingdom of heaven. Blessed are you when people insult you, persecute you and falsely say all kinds of evil against you because of me. Rejoice and be glad, because great is your reward in heaven, for in the same way they persecuted the prophets who were before you." *These are the Beatitudes.*

40. Matthew 6:9–13—"Our Father which art in heaven, hallowed be thy name. Thy kingdom come, thy will be done in earth, as it is in heaven. Give us this day our daily bread. And forgive us our debts, as we forgive our debtors. And lead us not into temptation, but deliver us from evil" (KJV). *If Jesus prayed this prayer, then we surely ought to.*

Acknowledgments

I must first give all praises to God for the things He has done to enhance my life's journey. On a daily basis I am reminded of His word where He says, "Now to him who is able to do immeasurably more than all we ask or imagine, according to his power that is at work within us, to him be glory in the church and in Christ Jesus throughout all generations, for ever and ever" (Ephesians 3:20–21), God, You've outdone Yourself when it comes to me. I will never be able to thank You enough!

Throughout my life's journey, He has put many people in my life (good and bad) to teach me life lessons, to love me, and to support and encourage me. This book has been a long time coming, and I have to thank my family and many friends for their unconditional love throughout this entire process.

I owe a debt of gratitude to my sons and daughters, who supported me when I made the decision to ultimately pursue my dream of going to college. They allowed me to lose the "Mommy" ties so that I could take some time to really discover just who Lucille is. They gave me the go-ahead to move forward toward my long-time goal to obtain a college degree. I give thanks to God for the two degrees that I have, and I now feel that I've made my children and fourteen grandchildren so very proud of me.

My babies, I cannot thank you enough for loving me unconditionally for real. Mommy and Grandma Cille loves you more than words can say. Thank you for the push and for the words I still hear echoing in my heart and ears every day when I am away from you that say, "You can do this."

I would also like to give thanks to my entire family. You all laid the strongest foundation that there could be for any family. You all surrounded me with the catalysts I needed to strive for a better life outside of Newark, New Jersey. I will always need your love and continued support—there is nothing like family.

I would be remiss if I did not thank Phillip Harrison (my only husband) for the twenty-eight years of love and adventure we shared. Thank you for taking me on adventures I never could have imagined as a young girl growing up in New Jersey. Although I grew up with you for many years, I grew away from you at a certain point in my life. Our ultimate separation enabled me to continue on my own life's journey. I'll never forget the life lessons you taught me, especially when you would remind me that "to stumble is not to fall." I learned so much from you, and I will always be grateful for the years we spent as a couple and the children we had together. Your strength did not waver during the worst times of our lives. For that, you will always hold a very special place in my heart. I remain . . . *my dear.*

To all the men in my life who have encouraged, inspired, and supported me through some of my most recent life changes, your presence has been invaluable to my growth. You've taught me so much about the ins and outs of relationships and how sometimes ending a relationship can lead to a more fulfilling one.

Many thanks to my special sister friends: Sandra Jeter, Martha Korman-Zumwalt, Charcey Glenn, Marie Jackson, Dassie Coleman, Janie Whitney, Anne Sealey, Letha Smith (deceased), Cathy Williams, Leah Wilcox, Sharon McMillan, Margaret Bonnett, and Pastor Gwen Lynch. You all are always there when I need you, and I feel your arms holding me up when I feel like I'm falling down. Sometimes a sista needs another listening ear too. I hope I have not worn your ears out yet. I love you, my sisters, my friends.

To the Mothers of Professional Basketball Players, Inc., who have allowed me to be the new voice and representative for you and our overall mission. I thank you for trusting me and having a great deal of confidence in me. I continue to have a sisterly love for all of you, and I sincerely thank you for your continued support as I live out our organization's mission in the Orlando community.

Special thanks to Lester Knispel and Dennis Roach, who always accept my calls, pray for me, and treat me with loving-kindness and constantly do what's needed to ensure that all of my business matters are done legally, with decency, and who ensure that all my affairs are in order. That's the way God planned it. Thank you for allowing me to use your staff, even as they continue to work very hard for you and Shaquille. You are all gems, and I love and appreciate you!

Cynthia Atterbury, Uncle Mike Parrish, Uncle Jerome Crawford, Joe Cavallero, Thomas "Mr. APC" Gosney, Uncle Albert Solomon, Donnie Wilson, and the entire Mine O'Mine family . . . I've got special love and appreciation for all of you guys! Thank you for being the world's best administrative staff, all-purpose employees, and security team. Thank you for guarding our family's integrity as well as our interests.

To Ms. Allison Samuels (my new friend and business associate), who listened to my words and inner thoughts. You worked tirelessly to put my feelings and words into plain English as I expressed them to you. Thanks for helping me share my journey with so many women who have been in the same place . . . a state of mental welfare. You listened as well as understood the joy and pain in my memoir and really asked the right questions to get the right answers. You're an expert in your craft, and I sincerely thank you for your patience and assistance. My son couldn't have chosen anyone better to help me get this project done. Thank you, girl!

Folio Literary Management and Steve Troha, what can I say? You all took a chance on me! Steven, from the moment we first met, you instantly reminded me of my own sons who work hard to get a job done. The way you put your heart into this project for me showed me how much you cared about my story. I thank you for caring—you are phenomenal. I am grateful to you for all that you did to help make my dream a reality. Your efforts to shop my story in the publishing world made a difference. I owe you one!

I would also like to thank Nicole Childers for making sure that all the i's were dotted and all the t's were crossed. Thank you for helping my story sing!

A special thanks to Gilda Squire for helping me shine.

Finally, to my publisher, Joel Miller, thank you for truly visualizing the picture I tried to paint in your office that day. And to Kristen Parrish—many thanks for seeing this all the way through. To the rest of the staff at Thomas Nelson Publishing, I just can't thank you enough for taking a chance on me. This is my first project, and I pray we can do many other projects together. Working on this book with you has been the experience of a lifetime. I offer a sincere thanks to you for your support, and I thank you for giving me the ability to bring people happiness with your literary works in the world's publishing arena. Without knowing it, you helped me realize a lifelong dream of becoming a published author. Your actions spoke much louder than your words, and I am eternally grateful for that! Gratitude is something that I'll never be able to express enough. Thank you, thank you, thank you, thank you!

The Odessa Chambliss
Quality of Life Fund

When my mother died of ovarian cancer in 1996, we knew so little about the disease, I'm ashamed to say. For generations in the African-American community, and possibly in many others, talking about health issues, especially those that were connected to a woman's reproductive system, was off-limits. Back then, shame and embarrassment were attached to anything regarding our bodies and the organs inside that made us women.

Years ago, even breast cancer carried a certain negative stigma with it, before education, information, and books became available to educate the masses. I always felt that my mother suffered in silence for years with ovarian cancer because she didn't want to discuss her "female problems" with anyone, including our family. Neither my sisters nor I knew the extent of her pain and illness until it was far too advanced to do anything about it. But that was over ten years ago. Today there are endless Web sites, research centers, and books available that discuss the fact that ovarian cancer is the fifth-leading cause of death among women. According to the American Cancer Society in 2008, more than 21,000 women were diagnosed with ovarian cancer, and about 15,520 women died of the disease.

Though my mother did suffer in silence for far too long, ovarian cancer can be very difficult to diagnose. Its symptoms can mimic bladder and digestive disorders and a host of other health problems. Since there is no effective screening test for ovarian cancer to date, my hope is that women educate themselves about the disease, listen to their bodies, and make a point of getting tested every year. With an early diagnosis, a woman has a 90 percent chance of survival. A woman's lifetime risk of ovarian cancer is 1 in 67.

My brother and sisters founded the Odessa Chambliss Quality of Life Fund the year of my mother's death, with several ideas in mind. First and foremost, we hoped to honor our mother, who loved us with all her heart. She fought so bravely for her life. We also vowed to use this fund to provide grant supplementation for individuals pursuing a career in nursing, and to assist those students who require incidentals, such as medical supplies, laptop computers, and necessities that are not assessible through basic tuitions. Additionally, this fund will provide monetary scholarships for education and cancer research at institutions and facilities that identify an urgent need for assistance.

Each year, we hold an annual event in Orlando called Shaq's Mama Said Knock You Out, which raises the bulk of the money for the fund. Each year, Shaquille and his NBA buddies host and attend our annual golf tournament, gala, and silent auction.

To date, we've raised over a million dollars for the fund, and our hope is that those numbers continue to grow. Cancer has had a devastating presence in my life, with both my mother and my daughter (who survived and is thriving), so I plan to continue fighting this disease until the day it stops taking lives and breaking hearts.

Donations to the fund can be sent to:

Odessa Chambliss Quality of Life Fund
6130 Foxfield Court
Windermere, FL 34786

A Note from Lucille

When I look at the homeless, I say, "That could have been me." When I look at the depressed, I say, "That could have been me." When I look at the faces of the terminally ill, I say, "That could have been me."

For so long I was looking for my purpose in life, and I would wonder, "Why me, God. Why me?"

During this journey I've come to realize that there is a reason for everything, and without a test there is no testimony. I am living my testimony, and my purpose is to share it while I live it. I am on an assignment, and so are all of you. Through all of my trials and tests, God has remained faithful, and He has never left me. Because of that, I try my best to be a woman of unwavering faith and stay obedient to God's direction and solutions for victorious living.

My Favorite Songs

1. "Why I Sing" (Kirk Franklin)
2. "No Weapon" (Fred Hammond)
3. "The Battle Is Not Yours" (Yolanda Adams)
4. "Let's Dance" (Hezekiah Walker)
5. "I Won't Complain" (Rev. Paul Jones)
6. "Just a Prayer Away" (Yolanda Adams)
7. "Finally" (Helen Baylor)
8. "Stand" (Donnie McClurkin)
9. "Make Me Real" (Dorinda Clark Cole)
10. "We Need a Word from the Lord" (Vickie Winans)
11. "Angels Watching Over Me" (Virtue)
12. "For Every Mountain" (Kurt Carr)
13. "You're Next in Line for a Miracle" (Shirley Caesar)
14. "He'll Meet My Need" (T. D. Jakes and the Potter's House Mass Choir)
15. "Let Go" (DeWayne Woods)
16. "Never Would Have Made It" (Marvin Sapp)
17. "Try" (Kim Burrell and Marvin Winans)
18. "Blessed and Highly Favored" (The Clark Sisters)

The *mental wealth* I own and experience today is more precious than any amount of money I could ever have. And in my life, I've been exposed to some of the most opulent lifestyles a person could ever imagine. But those things mean little to nothing to me without God.

Although I seem gentle and low-key in person, I know that I am strong and courageous because of what I've been through. Let me be the one to remind you, as my mother always used to remind me, that *God has the master plan.* Today, I take full responsibility for many of my past mistakes because I was in a state of mental welfare.

What do you know about taking responsibility? Know that it works sometimes like a two-sided coin: Responsibilty/Rewards. Taking responsibility can mean three things: (a) recognizing what you're responsible for, (b) recognizing who you're responsible to, and (c) acting responsible at all times.

You can give all the excuses you want, but this does not clear you of accepting responsibility for yourself and your actions. Be honest and true to yourself, and if you feel that your life is not going in the direction you'd like it to . . . take responsibility to change it!

You can start the change process by making up your mind to change your attitude (adopt a can-do attitude), which I know for a fact will change your present circumstances. After that attitude adjustment, next comes believing in yourself—there is no mental wealth without this!

When speaking to young men and women, I remind them that believing in themselves, coupled with having faith in their own ability, are two of the key ingredients needed to stay in a good place, a mental wealth state. Martin Luther King Jr. once said that "faith is taking a step when you don't see the whole staircase." Think of yourself as the most beautiful flower in the garden, and have a little faith that you will grow more and more beautiful! Dream and dream BIG! Another thing, when you begin to visualize your dreams, desires, wishes, and hopes, before you know it, time will have passed and your dream will have taken on life and become a reality.

Ever since I was young I wanted to be a motivational speaker, and I worked very hard to get to this point . . . and now here I am, doing the very thing that I love to do—talk while making it a point to say something that will encourage somebody! Now, picture yourself in a leadership position: While your peers are sitting, you will concentrate on STANDING; while your peers are standing, you will stand tall and STAND OUT; while your peers stand out, you will be the one OUTSTANDING. And as a result of your mental wealth state, you will be the example by which all other standards will be measured!

I want everyone reading this book to know that today all of us are in a special place if we are alive and breathing. I don't claim to know all there is to know about life, or to be a perfect parent/grandparent either, but I have to say to the children out there, listen to your parents, and know they love you.

To the parents, don't come down too hard on your children, because you can crush their delicate spirits. Remember to have a level of respect for your children, and let them have a voice. You might be surprised at what you may learn by just listening to a child speak.

I encourage you to work together and keep the communication lines open within the family structure. Look at your children as flowers in a garden that need to be watered and loved to grow. In other words, pay attention to everything they say and all that they do. Their lives may depend on it.

Young people face tremendous peer pressure these days, and we as parents have to understand that their lives today are nothing like ours were as children. Be patient, be firm, and present for them, no matter what. You'll be surprised at what just being there for your children means to them. I wasn't always a perfect parent to Shaquille, Lateefah, Ayesha, and Jamal, but I was always there for them, and I know that's helped make them become the adults I've always prayed they'd be.